THEODORE M. DAVIS'
EXCAVATIONS: BIBÂN EL MOLÛK

THE TOMB OF QUEEN TÎYI

INTRODUCTION TO THE 1990 SECOND EDITION
THE ARCHAEOLOGICAL ANALYSIS OF KV 55
1907–1990
AND
A SELECT BIBLIOGRAPHY OF KV 55 LITERATURE
BY
NICHOLAS REEVES

THE DISCOVERY OF THE TOMB
BY
THEODORE M. DAVIS

SKETCH OF THE LIFE OF QUEEN TÎYI
BY
GASTON MASPERO

NOTE ON THE ESTIMATE OF THE AGE ATTAINED BY THE PERSON
WHOSE SKELETON WAS FOUND IN THE TOMB
BY
G. ELLIOT SMITH, M.A., M.D., F.R.S.
PROFESSOR OF ANATOMY IN THE EGYPTIAN GOVERNMENT SCHOOL OF MEDICINE, CAIRO

THE EXCAVATIONS OF 1907
BY
EDWARD AYRTON

CATALOGUE OF THE OBJECTS DISCOVERED
BY
GEORGE DARESSY

ILLUSTRATIONS
BY
E. HAROLD JONES

KMT COMMUNICATIONS
SAN FRANCISCO
1990

SECOND EDITION
© *KMT Communications, San Francisco, 1990*
ISBN 1-879388-00-6 Hardcover
ISBN 1-879388-01-4 Softcover

CONTENTS

―――――

LIST OF ILLUSTRATIONS

PREFACE TO THE SECOND EDITION

THE prospect of republishing the *Theodore M. Davis's Excavations: Bibán el Molâk* series was suggested by Oriental Institute Museum archivist John A. Larson, in a note to his two-part article, "Theodore M. Davis and the So-Called Tomb of Queen Tiye," appearing in the spring and summer 1990 numbers of *KMT*. Originally put into print in London by Archibald Constable and Co., Ltd., all six folio-sized volumes in the series have been long in the public domain, making such second editions possible. Copies of the Davis originals are difficult to locate outside institutional collections; and, when one of these volumes does come onto the used-book market, its price is very considerable ($450 as of late 1990). Thus, KMT Communications of San Francisco has undertaken the project of making these Egyptological "classics" readily available once again, in an affordable new edition, in both hardcover and softbound versions.

Although not the first of the *Bibán el Molâk* volumes, *The Tomb of Queen Tîyi* is the obvious choice to begin the Second Edition series, because this "official" account of one of Egyptology's most problematic discoveries has been a source of scholarly controversy since it first came off press eighty years ago.

As his Introduction to the present *Tîyi* edition, Nicholas Reeves presents a history of the archaeological analysis of the Davis/Aryton find and of the ongoing debate regarding the identity of the skeletal royal occupant of Kings Valley Tomb 55 (the so-called Tomb of Queen Tiye, also known as the Amarna Cache and KV 55). Dr. Reeves, himself a recent participant in this dialogue, studied ancient history at University College London, and received his doctorate in Egyptology from the University of Durham. A curator in the Department of Egyptian Antiquities at the British Museum, London, he has written extensively on the history and archaeology of Egypt, including his books *Valley of the Kings: the decline of the royal necropolis* and *The Complete Tutankhamun* (both London, 1990). Dr. Reeves has also compiled an annotated bibliography of select Tomb 55 literature, which follows his introductory essay. It should prove to be a valuable resource for students of the Amarna and immediate post-Amarna periods, for whom the KV 55 controversy never wears thin.

This republication of *Tîyi* is slightly revised: A short section of irrelevant material in the original edition has been excluded (the "Brief Summary of the Objects Found in the Tomb of Queen Tauosrît"), as this was appended to his text by Davis without explanation and invariably puzzles first-time *Tîyi* readers. (It is a preliminary list of pieces brought to light during Davis's investigation of KV 56 shortly before his Tomb 55 report went to press and will be included in the appropriate *Bibán el Molâk* volume.)

Likewise, Davis's one-sentence "Preface" to the original edition, which occupied an entire page by itself, has been left out of the Second Edition for sake of economy. It read, "I desire to express my gratitude to Dr. Professor Schafer, of Berlin, for allowing me to publish the beautiful 'Head of an Unknown Queen.' Theodore M. Davis, Newport, Rhode Island, U.S.A."

Also, the republished *Tîyi* plates are numbered differently from the first arrangement; included are five images not found in the 1910 edition (pls. II, XXXVIII, XXXIX). These numbering changes have been made to illustration references within the volume's text. Lastly, the few tinted "illustrations in colour" of the original (pls. XXXIII, XXXIV, XXXV, XXXVII) are reproduced as monochromes in this Second Edition.

Dennis C. Forbes
KMT Communications
San Francisco, 1990

INTRODUCTION

THE ARCHAEOLOGICAL ANALYSIS OF KV 55
1907–1990

NICHOLAS REEVES © 1990

THE *Tomb of Queen Tîyi*—of which the present volume is a second edition—was first published in 1910 as the official account of what has become Egyptology's most controversial archaeological find: that of the Amarna royal burial discovered in 1907 by Theodore M. Davis in Tomb KV 55 in the Valley of the Kings. The publication was a lavish, multi-authored production, with contributions from some of the leading Egyptological lights of the day: philologist and historian Gaston Maspero, anatomist Grafton Elliot Smith, archaeologist Edward Russell Ayrton, Cairo Museum curator Georges Daressy, and artist Ernest Harold Jones. Yet, as a record of discovery, it failed dismally. Its mix of fact, assumption, error and omission has baffled scholars for more than eighty years, and obscures still a wholly convincing identification of the Tomb 55 occupant and a full understanding of the deposit in which the remains were found.

Much of the blame for the book's shortcomings must rest with Davis himself, who edited the volume. The involvement in archaeology of this retired New York lawyer began innocuously enough when, in 1902, he gave money to the Egyptian Antiquities Service for excavations to be carried out in his name in the New Kingdom royal burial ground on the west bank at Luxor. The work was supervised by the Egyptian government's inspector-general of antiquities for Upper Egypt, Howard Carter, and resulted in the discovery of the small shaft-tomb of Userhat (KV 45) and a box containing two leather loincloths from above the tomb of the fan-bearer Maiherpri (KV 36). Because of the season's success, the sponsorship arrangement was renewed each year until 1905. Work continued to be supervised by Carter, followed, for a short time in 1904–05, by J.E. Quibell; thanks to the efforts of the inspectors of the Antiquities Service, Davis was to build a reputation for himself as the man who found a new tomb every season.

Excavating for this millionaire American amateur became a distraction the hard-pressed Antiquities Service could do without, however, and in 1905 Davis was persuaded by Arthur Weigall, the new chief inspector for the district, to employ his own archaeologist. Davis readily agreed; and, in October of that same year, Edward R. Ayrton, an experienced member of the Egypt Exploration Fund's team at Deir el-Bahri, took up his post as Davis's new field director (pl. II). And it was Ayrton, during his second season for Davis, who stumbled upon Tomb 55.

The young archaeologist found himself in a very different position from the government inspectors who had preceded him, and from the start was left in no doubt as to who was calling the tune. Nonetheless, Davis's autocratic manner did not prevent Ayrton from carrying out his work in as complete a manner as circumstances would allow. During the clearance of KV 55, notes were taken, measurements made, sketches produced and photographs shot; the terms of Davis's concession stipulated all of this as a minimal requirement for the report which the excavator had to submit to the Antiquities Service (a report which perhaps languishes still in the archives of that organization). But the *publication* of such archaeological detail was another matter. This interested Davis not at all—to the detriment of Ayrton's reputation, which has suffered considerably from the fact that his professional contributions to the 1910 *Tîyi* volume were heavily edited by Davis or else omitted altogether.

Because of the book's tantalizingly vague archaeological coverage, much effort has been expended over the years on filling in its many gaps from a close scrutiny of the several unofficial accounts of the discovery which have, by a happy chance, come down to us. Ayrton published at the time two brief, independent descriptions of the find [12]*; Arthur Weigall, the Antiquities Service inspector, over the years wrote [76–79] and lectured widely on the discovery; while Gaston Maspero, director-general of the Antiquities Service, also penned essays on the tomb and its contents [46–49]. Less extensive accounts exist by Howard Carter (among his notes preserved in the Griffith Institute in Oxford) [55], and, in published form, by the archaeologist C.T. Currelly [20] and the artist Walter Tyndale [75]. Other eye-witnesses, such as Emma B. Andrews [45, 81], Davis's cousin and mistress, and the artist Joseph Lindon Smith, kept diaries (those of the latter subsequently written up in book form [71]); and we have, in addition, one or two letters written by the artist Harold Jones [15] and by Davis himself [55]. When these various strands of evidence are combined, a rather more coherent picture of the discovery emerges.

As the diary of Mrs. Andrews reveals, the entrance to KV 55 was uncovered by Ayrton on Sunday, the 6th of January, 1907, in the central part of the Valley, a few meters to the west of (and overlain by chippings quarried from) the tomb of Ramesses IX; it was brought to Davis's attention on Monday the 7th. Three days before, on the 3rd of January, "a recess in the rock" (now designated KV C) had been found immediately above the tomb entrance. The precise nature of KV C is not at all clear; though its "several large jars of the XXth dynasty type" are not catalogued in the *Tîyi* volume, they perhaps represented a cache of embalming materials associated with Tomb 55 below [55], similar to that associated with the Tutankhamun burial which Davis later recovered from pit KV 54 on the 21st of December, 1907.

KV 55 proper was first entered by Ayrton, Davis, J.L. Smith and Weigall, as Antiquities Service representative, on the morning of the 9th of January. The

---

*See listing in "A Select Bibliography of Tomb 55" following the "Introduction" (p. 19). All other bracketed numbers refer to "Bibliography" listings. ED.

examination of the find continued the following day, with Smith starting work on producing watercolour sketches of the interior; and on the 11th, a photographer, R. Paul, arrived from Cairo to record the burial in position before clearance began. Maspero arrived in Luxor the following Monday, the 14th of January; the Assyriologist A.H. Sayce appeared on the 18th, viewing the tomb with the German Egyptologist Alfred Wiedemann on the 19th. By January 20th C.T. Currelly was on the scene, together (presumably) with Walter Tyndale and the member of Parliament for Birmingham (England), Sir Benjamin Stone, equipped with his camera. And Tuesday, January 22nd, saw the arrival of Harold Jones—a young artist lured away from John Garstang's excavations at Abydos to prepare drawings for Davis of the shrine panels (pls. XXXIII–XXXV).

At the mouth of the tomb, the excavators encountered remains of the original cemented door-blocking; this had been plastered on its outer surface and stamped with the jackal-and-nine-captives seal (and, according to Weigall, "the seal of Tutankhamon" [78], though this remains open to question). This blocking had been partially dismantled in ancient times, and the entrance closed off with a loosely built wall of limestone resting upon the rubble fill of the stairway beyond. The tomb's secondary blocking had itself been breached, giving access to a sloping corridor partially filled with limestone chippings which flowed out into the tomb's single chamber.

As the *in situ* photographs taken by Paul and published in the *Tîyi* volume (pls. XXVI–XXXII) show, on top of the corridor rubble fill lay one panel and a single door-leaf of what proved to be a large, gilded wooden shrine. Further dismantled elements from this same funerary structure—which had been prepared for Queen Tiye's burial by her son, Akhenaten, and which carried representations of the royal pair offering to the disc—were found at the end of the corridor, as well as arranged around the walls in the northern half of the tomb chamber. The heretic's figure and cartouches had everywhere on this shrine been carefully erased in antiquity. In the southern part of the tomb was a decayed wooden coffin adorned with crook and flail and carrying an uninscribed bronze uraeus; within the coffin was a nameless mummy. The cartouches in the coffin's principal texts had been cut out, and the sheet-gold of its face mask had been brutally torn away below the eyes. Within a large niche (an unfinished side-room) in the south wall were four calcite canopic jars with portrait-head stoppers, their uraei snapped off and their identifying inscriptions chiseled away (the latter, it transpires, before the jars' deposition). Four mud "magical bricks" of Akhenaten, two inscribed in hieroglyphs, two in hieratic, were scattered to the four cardinal points among the debris, together with the remains of a number of wooden boxes, which spilled their contents—for the most part minor funerary objects of faience and stone, some inscribed with the names of Amenophis III and Tiye—out onto the chamber floor. Other pieces would, in due course, be recovered from the debris as it was sifted by Ayrton, including a large uraeus of gilded bronze, perhaps from a statue, inscribed with the early form of the Aten's cartouches.

As soon as the find had been photographed, Ayrton began the ticklish job of clearing the deposit for transfer to Cairo. The corridor was gradually emptied, with the shrine elements suspended on timber supports. Between January 21st–23rd, attempts were made to secure the detached gilded gesso of the shrine panels with washes of varnish and applications of paraffin wax; on Wednesday, January 23rd, Mrs. Andrews records Jones's difficulty in copying the scenes of the shrine, which were falling to pieces before his eyes, and she notes that the decision was made "to take an impression of inscriptions by wax and plaster of paris" [81]. The extent to which this last desperate action—which Mrs. Andrews may well have misunderstood or misrepresented—contributed to the present gesso-free state of the few surviving panels of the shrine woodwork is not recorded. According to a letter from Davis to Weigall, dated 29 January 1908 [55], plans were being made a year later to move the panels still resting within the chamber to allow Jones to complete his copies—which would imply that at least some of the gilded-gesso decoration was still in place at that later date.

On Friday, January 25th, 1907, the excavators' attentions were turned to the coffin, the collapsed and dislodged lid of which was successfully lifted in sections though the water-rotted base appears to have already crumbled away into its component inlays. Beneath the coffin were the decayed remains of a lion-bier of gilded wood; and when the debris of this was eventually cleared, a number of small clay seal-impressions was found. Only recently has a photograph of these sealings, some among them bearing the names of Amenophis III and Tutankhamun, been brought to light [55] (pl. XXXVIII).

According to his version of events [71], Joseph Lindon Smith was entrusted with the task of dismantling the badly rotted mummy *in situ*, in the presence of Davis, Maspero, Emma Andrews, Weigall, Ayrton, Jones and Smith's wife, Corinna. Upon the mummy—according to Maspero "somewhat scantily swathed in two or three wrappings of linen, fine in texture but very worn" [48]—lay the gold lining-sheets of the coffin lid. When these had been removed, the body could be clearly seen, its left arm crossed over the chest (a characteristically female pose), and, like the extended right arm, adorned with three gold-foil bracelets. The head (which had broken away from the body when struck by a rock in antiquity) was "crowned" with a displaced vulture pectoral of thin sheet gold, which when raised revealed the badly damaged skull. This was in turn lifted out of the coffin by Smith and placed in a basket held by Ayrton—a basket to which the other bones would later be added, sealed and sent on to Cairo (despite Mrs. Andrews' belief that the body would be left in the tomb), together with two fragmentary text bands from the coffin (pl. XXXIX).

As Smith felt through the bandages of the chest for the loose beads of a broad collar, the mummy "crumbled into ashes and sifted down through the bones" into the shallow pool of water in which the coffin lay. Collecting the pieces of this collar (other elements of which would be stolen by Davis's workmen, to find their way, via Howard Carter, from the Luxor antiquities market into Davis's personal collection and eventual sale at Sotheby's in New York in 1976 [72]), Smith also recovered a further coffin-lining sheet, inscribed with the cartouche of Akhenaten.

What was the nature of this confused deposit, in which the names of Tiye and Akhenaten were so inextricably mixed? It was a question to which there would be no easy answer. Davis, basing himself upon the evident owner of the shrine, thrilled at the possiblity of having found the burial of Queen Tiye, the powerful and influential wife of Pharaoh Amenophis III; and he at first accepted as hers the coffined body and the four calcite canopic jars. Maspero was more cautious, believing that the deposit was a reburial and that the funerary furnishings belonged to at least two persons [71]. Both he and Weigall [77–79] inclined strongly to the view that, while the shrine did indeed belong to Tiye, the coffin, decayed human remains and canopic jars were those of Akhenaten. Two visiting physicians who examined the skeletal mummy for Davis had early on concurred that the bones were definitely those of a woman; while anatomist Elliot Smith, examining the skull and bones a few months later in Cairo, identified them as those of a young man with wide hips, a pendent chin and distorted cranium brought on by "chronic hydrocephalus"—Akhenaten to a tee. Yet the age at death of the skeleton, according to Smith, was around twenty-five or twenty-six years, perhaps with a little leeway on either side, but, on the whole, too low for it to be that of the heretic king. Maspero's answer was that some confusion had occurred at the time the body was transferred to the KV 55 cache; one possibility, he proposed (perhaps following a suggestion of Norman de Garis Davies), would be to see the body as that of Akhenaten's supposed son-in-law and successor, the enigmatic Smenkhkare [48]. Davis was unaffected, one way or the other; for him, whatever the sex of the occupant, the tomb was that of Queen Tiye—and that is how he titled his book.

Even when *The Tomb of Queen Tîyi* appeared in 1910, therefore, there was little overall consensus, and a study of the KV 55 coffin published in 1916 by Georges Daressy [21] complicated the matter still further. Daressy's interpretation of the texts on the coffin (bands B and C of which were stolen from Elliot Smith's laboratory, to surface years later on the European antiquities market [55], pl. XXXIX) seemed to confirm that Akhenaten had been its intended occupant; but Daressy also observed that these texts had been subtly altered by the insertion of thin gold-foil patches carrying hieroglyphic signs which could only imply that the coffin had originally been prepared for a woman. Influenced by the presence of the queen's shrine within the Tomb 55 assemblage, Daressy concluded that this woman had been Tiye.

The identity of the mummy found within the coffin was a different matter: though this coffin had indubitably been altered for Akhenaten, the remains could not possibly be those of the heretic. Influenced, no doubt, by Elliot Smith's estimate of the age at death of the individual, which had been restated in Smith's *Catalogue général* description of 1912 [67], Daressy favoured the claims (now necessarily to be abandoned) of the then little-known Tutanhkamun—of whom, he felt, the canopic-jar portraits offered a strong likeness. (A mere three years later, these same jars would be re-identified by Heinrich Schäfer [61], on equally tenuous grounds, as portraits of Nefertiti, the wife of Akhenaten.)

In the meantime, further evidence was accumlating. Howard Carter, digging south of Tomb 55 in the course of his work for the fifth Earl of Carnarvon in 1921, brought to light yet more fragments from the deposit: a jasper burnisher and some copper-alloy rosette fragments from a funerary pall, pieces which had been dropped outside the tomb in antiquity [55]. Evidently dismissed by Carter as unimportant, no account was ever published of the finds, and their present whereabouts are unknown.

In 1922, an article was published by Weigall [79], in part a response to a study brought out by the German Egyptologist Kurt Sethe the previous year [64]. Weigall sought to reassert Akhenaten's claim to the Tomb 55 body, a claim which had been refuted by Sethe on the grounds of the low estimated-age-at-death of the skeleton, by arguing that the king might well have been as young as thirty when he died. This, for Weigall, was the obvious conclusion, since the mummy had been found in a coffin which "is that of Akhenaton without any question," and had been accompanied by what the former inspector believed were that king's canopic jars. According to Weigall, Akhenaten's mummy had been transferred from el-Amarna by agents of Tutankhamun and reburied at Thebes in the tomb of his mother, Tiye, from which tomb, now polluted by the heretic's presence, the queen's body was later removed.

Weigall's thesis, as we shall consider, was not without its attractions, and a year or two later, in the wake of the Tutankhamun hysteria, Elliot Smith [68] sought to strengthen the identification of the KV 55 remains by drawing attention to the possibility that the peculiarly depicted Akhenaten had suffered from a disorder ("Dystocia [Dystrophia] adiposo-genitalis," or "Fröhlich's syndrome") which delayed normal skeletal development (specifically the union of the epiphyses). If this were so, Smith argued, the age at death of the Tomb 55 occupant could be increased by as much as a decade.

Although a diagnosis of adiposo-genital dystrophy would imply that Akhenaten had been impotent—a conclusion difficult to reconcile with his fathering of six daughters and at least one son—, many of Weigall's critics were mollified by Elliot Smith's proposal, and the attribution of the KV 55 individual to Akhenaten seems to have stood, generally (if uneasily) accepted, until 1931. In that year, Rex Engelbach [24] returned to the thorny question of the coffin's ownership and eventual occupant, prompted by Derry's 1923 review of the skeletal material; this review, though not published until 1931 [23], had turned Smith's conclusions on their head (literally), ruling out any possiblity of the hydrocephalus which might have supported his diagnosis and reducing the estimated age of the coffin's occupant still further, to twenty-three years. Engelbach questioned whether the inscriptions of the Tomb 55 coffin could possibly allow that it had originally been prepared for Tiye, as Daressy had suggested, since there was not enough space in the lacunae for the queen's titulary. Nor, for similar reasons of space, could the inscriptions have been altered from those of Nefertiti. The canopic jar lids, Engelbach further pointed out (following an observation made by Guy Brunton), had not originally carried uraei: these had been *additions* to the original design. Engelbach believed that both jars and coffin had been prepared for a person of non-royal status, and were only subsequently employed for a king. For him, this was one and the same person: the ephemeral prince Smenkhkare, for whom, as a private person, the equipment will have been first made and later altered, following his elevation to the throne. It was an identification clinched, for Engelbach, by the presence in the coffin's texts of the epithet "beloved of Waenre" (i.e. of Akhenaten), an integral component of the name of the heretic's successor. And Derry's new estimate of the KV 55 skeleton's age at death added considerable support to the equation.

Engelbach's reconstruction was not without its difficulties, and he returned to it in 1940 [26], though modifying his opinion only to the extent of admitting (without further elaboration) the possibility that the coffin might, indeed, have been prepared originally for a woman—perhaps Nefertiti, who at the time was held to have fallen from grace before Akhenaten's death. Others took a rather different view. For the Chicago Egyptologist Keith C. Seele [63], writing in 1955 and in effect concurring with much of what Engelbach had concluded, the obvious candidate was Akhenaten's second daughter, the prematurely deceased Meketaten; while for Cyril Aldred [1], writing in 1957, the claims of the eldest Amarna princess, Meritaten, were to be taken equally seriously.

Sir Alan Gardiner's inevitable contribution to the discussion came in 1957 [28]. His view, from a close study of the coffin's inscriptions, was that, irrespective of the apparent textual alterations (for which he was able to offer no explanation), its owner had "from first to last" been Akhenaten, an attribution confirmed for Gardiner by the presence in the tomb of the four "magical bricks" inscribed for that king. Gardiner was led to this conclusion by his belief that the speech on the foot of the coffin had been authored by Nefertiti, whose name had been expunged, he believed, at the time of her supposed "disgrace." Yet Weigall's theory that the tomb had originally contained the burial of Tiye, Gardiner found difficult to credit, since so few traces of her supposed occupancy had survived. In Gardiner's opinion, the el-Amarna royal tomb had been mercilessly ravaged a short time after Akhenaten's burial, and what remained—including the shrine of Tiye, the coffin of Akhenaten and the mummy which was believed to be that of the king—was gathered up for transfer to Thebes and safe reinterment there. Gardiner returned to the question in his review of Joseph Lindon Smith's *Tombs, Temples and Ancient Art* in 1959 [29]—here, like Engelbach, Seele and Aldred before him, to allow for the possibility that the coffin had originally been made for one of the Amarna princesses, to whose lesser status the fine though not superb coffin would have been better suited.

Gardiner was not alone in his interest in KV 55, and, to the extent that he believed the coffin to have been intended from the start for a king, his views coincided with those expressed in a paper by Günther Roeder which appeared at about the same time [57]. But for Roeder this king was Smenkhkare, as Engelbach had proposed, rather than Akhenaten. Moreover, the gold-foil patches on the coffin were evidence, not of a change of ownership, but of corrections made necessary by the work of a careless scribe.

Further discussion was to follow, with separate articles by H.W. Fairman [27] and Cyril Aldred [2] appearing in a single issue of the *Journal of Egyptian Archaeology* in 1961. Drawing attention to the inscription on two fragmentary calcite cosmetic jars of a secondary wife of Akhenaten, Kiya, in the Metropolitan Museum of Art in New York and in the British Museum in London, Fairman demonstrated the correctness of Gardiner's conclusion that the excised cartouches of the coffin must have contained the name of Akhenaten himself. However, "Since...it was deemed essential to change the words that in all five strips originally preceded the name and titulary of Akhenaten into epithets that beyond all doubt refer to a king, it is certain that the original text must have referred to a person who was not a king, for otherwise there would have been no obvious need to change the wording." Two candidates were put forward by Fairman as the original owner: Kiya herself, or Meritaten—Fairman's preference being for Meritaten, on the (erroneous) grounds that her inscriptions would better fit the available spaces in the coffin texts. The owner of the coffin, in its final form, however, will have been Smenkhkare (as Engelbach had proposed) and his, rather than Akhenaten's, the body found within it. The evidence of the "magical bricks," Fairman was inclined to discount because of the inappropriateness for Akhenaten of the epithet "the Osiris," and what he believed to be some uncertainty in the reading of the bricks' cartouches.

As is indicated by the title of his paper, "The tomb of Akhenaten at Thebes," Aldred took a very different view. For Aldred, the Tomb 55 coffin was in design that of a woman, who was not, however, a queen. Aldred's candidate, like Fairman's was Meritaten, though he, like Weigall before him, discerned in the Tomb 55 debris the burial of Akhenaten in the princess's coffin, with appropriately altered texts. The Smenkhkare connection, Aldred suggested, was a fiction, since the epithet "beloved of Waenre," without cartouche, might as easily have been applied to any member of the Amarna royal family. Aldred and the Glasgow pathologist A.T. Sandison [4, 59] sought to explain the apparent youthfulness of the coffin's occupant by positing (from a study of the king's peculiar physique, as reflected in the monuments of his reign) that Akhenaten suffered from a disorder of the pituitary gland—pituitary cranial dysplasia—displaying acromegaloid changes to the skull and face, changes which would have masked his true age at death. Aldred developed the thesis by examining the archaeological context of the deposit, following on from Weigall's view that Tomb 55 originally held two burials. Aldred stressed the importance of the relative positions of the shrine and coffin, concluding that "On the whole, the most likely event is that Akhenaten and Tiye were laid to rest in the tomb side by side and the queen was later removed elsewhere."

In spite of Aldred's well-argued reconstruction of events, Fairman's view that the body belonged to Smenkhkare seemed to find confirmation in the results of R.G. Harrison's re-examination of the Tomb 55 skeletal material published in 1966 [33]. This examination essentially confirmed the results of Derry's examination, reduced the estimated age at death still further, to between twenty and twenty-five years, and revealed no evidence of the postulated delay in maturation. D.J. Kidd's reconstruction of the facial features [33] of the broken skull appeared to offer additional proof that the remains could not possibly be those of Akhenaten: as restored, the face (so far as it resembled anyone) seemed to resemble Tutankhamun, Smenkhkare's putative younger brother. And further support for Harrison's results appeared in 1978 with Pedro Costa's comments on the skull's frontal sinuses [18]: the bones were undoubtedly male, with no evidence of acromegaly.

It was not until 1967 that the first cracks began to appear in the Fairman view of things, with publication by the Russian Egyptologist I.I. Perepelkin of a painstaking analysis of the extant corpus of Amarna inscriptions [50]—though Perepelkin's views received little currency in the west until the translation of his semi-popular *Secret of the Gold Coffin* [51] a decade later. Vindicating Daressy's original view that the KV 55 coffin had originally been prepared for a woman, Perepelkin was able to demonstrate that the recurring phraseology of its texts formed part of a titulary unique to the obscure secondary wife of Akhenaten, Kiya, whose claims Fairman had dismissed a few years before. (The German Egyptologist R. Hanke was to reach a similar conclusion, independently of Perepelkin, in an article published in 1975 [31]—except that Hanke wished to recognize in Kiya none other than the great royal wife Nefertiti.) According to Perepelkin, Kiya had been the original owner of the KV 55 canopic jars also (a view supported by this writer in 1981 [55] from an examination of the surviving traces of the erased texts, and since demonstrated by R. Krauss [42], *contra* G.T. Martin [45]), and the lids of these jars evidently offer four portraits of her. Kiya, therefore, had been the original owner of one of the principal groups of objects from the tomb; but the alterations to the texts of the coffin, the erasure of the texts on the jars and the addition of a uraeus to the brow of each jar's portrait-lid, as well as the evident sex of the body itself, all showed clearly that, in the end, it had not been she who had employed them. The intended occupant of Kiya's coffin was to have been a king—and this king, according to those portions of the text which survived, was Akhenaten, though the adaptations in question could only have been made some years after his death. Nevertheless, Perepelkin was forced by the anatomical data to concede that the mummy found within this coffin was *not* that of Akhenaten, but the body of Smenkhkare.

The present writer, whose discussions of KV 55 appeared in 1981 [53], 1982 [54] and, in a slightly revised form, in 1990 [55], has taken a rather different line. The finds from the tomb have been studied in conjunction with a schematic reconstruction of the deposit as it lay at the time of the discovery (a reconstruction now improved upon and up-dated in a forthcoming paper by Martha Bell [14]). From the manner in which the deposit lay, it has been possible to demonstrate that Tomb 55 represented the remains not of one but of two quite distinct reburials, made following the abandonment of the royal necropolis at el-Amarna—to judge from the seals employed, during the reign of Tutankhamun—with each burial positioned in a separate part of the chamber.

The first occupant of the tomb appears to have been Queen Tiye, whose gilded shrine, set up around her coffined mummy, originally occupied the centre of the Tomb 55 chamber, with boxes of funerary equipment ranged around. Following the installation of her burial, the corridor of Tomb 55 was filled with rubble, the entrance closed with a plastered stone wall and this blocking then stamped over its entire surface with the royal necropolis seal—the jackal couchant upon nine bound captives.

The second interment within KV 55 seems to have been introduced somewhat hurriedly a short time after that of Tiye, and to have included the altered Kiya/ Akhenaten coffin and its occupant, Kiya's adapted canopic jars, and the Akhenaten "magical bricks." In order to allow this material to be taken into the tomb, the plastered entrance-blocking had to be partially dismantled and the corridor fill pushed down into the chamber. The coffined body was then placed upon its bier amid this rubble, relegated to the northern edge of the chamber (because of Tiye's occupancy of the main area of the tomb); the magical bricks were casually tossed in the direction of the four cardinal points; and the canopic jars were positioned in the rough-hewn "niche"—which, in the original design of the tomb, had been intended as the beginning of a second chamber. The entrance was then closed off once again by erecting a dry-stone wall upon a foundation of the corridor fill.

The latest phase of activity within the tomb can be dated with some confidence to the reign of Rameses IX [55]: during the quarrying of the southwest side-chamber of this tomb, which overlies KV 55, the rock evidently began to sound hollow, drawing the tomb cutters' attention to the presence of the forgotten burial below. Work was stopped for them to explore—and what the Valley quarrymen found horrified them, to judge from what they did: the lower part of the exposed coffin's face was ripped away, depriving its occupant of air and sustenance; the eye inlays were prised out, blinding him; the canopic jar uraei were broken off, denying their owner divine protection and kingly status; and all instances of Akhenaten's name which could be found within the tomb by the workmen—including all but one of those of the coffin, then still intact as J.R. Harris has observed [55]—were excised. It may also be speculated that this same investigating party was responsible for hurling the stone which crushed the front of the mummy's skull.

Tiye's shrine was next dismantled (in a somewhat rough-and-ready manner, one of its jammed bronze tenons having to be cut through with a chisel) and her coffined body and much of her funerary equipment then removed from the "polluting presence" of the desecrated kingly mummy, for reburial elsewhere (eventually to turn up in the Amenophis II cache in 1898, if we are to believe the identification of the "Elder Lady" proposed by J.E. Harris). During the course of this transfer, a few small elements of the queen's funerary equipment were accidentally dropped outside the tomb, to be recovered by Carter in 1921. As for the shrine itself, a start was made on "censoring" its scenes—hacking out the heretic's image and replacing ("in red ink") the name of Akhenaten with that of Amenophis III—in an attempt to make it fit for removal with the queen. But it was soon found that the large side panels could not be manoeuvred up the only partially cleared corridor—and so the shrine's several sections were abandoned, and the tomb entrance covered over once again, to remain hidden until that early-January day in 1907.

In many respects, the archaeological analysis of KV 55 has come full circle. It appears that the tomb *was* that of Tiye (albeit a reburial of the queen), to which a second mummy was later introduced before Tiye herself was removed; while—

despite James P. Allen's recent and ingenious textual reconstruction [8], which argues that the coffin had been adapted for a son of Akhenaten—the sum of the archaeological and inscriptional data seems to indicate that the abused and abandoned KV 55 mummy *was* that of the heretic himself, as Weigall long ago proposed. Were it not for the estimated age at death of the remains, this latter identification would by now have been accepted fact for more than eighty years—and we are amply justified in asking how precise such estimates actually are. It is a question only the anatomists can answer, but there are signs of a lessening of confidence from both within and outside the profession—doubts which are perhaps reflected in the most recent age-at-death estimate proposed for the Tomb 55 skeleton, by Hussien and Harris [39], of thirty-five years. Further details of this latest study, and of the implications of the new skull-reconstruction [40], are awaited with keen interest. If the results of the examination prove any more reliable than those that have gone before, it seems that the burden of proof will, for the first time, lie with those seeking to attribute the body to anyone other than Akhenaten himself.

That at least, is the direction in which the evidence at present seems to point—but it is a brave man who would venture that the last word on this problematic burial has yet been said. With Davis's thought-provoking report once again readily here at hand, it is a controversy which readers are now able, and will no doubt wish, to explore further for themselves.

Nicholas Reeves
October 1990

A SELECT BIBLIOGRAPHY OF TOMB 55

Abbreviations

ASAE	Annales du Service des Antiquités de l'Égypte
BHM	Bulletin of the History of Medicine
BIFAO	Bulletin de l'Institut français d'archéologie orientale du Caire
BMMA	Bulletin of the Metropolitan Museum of Art
CAH	Cambridge Ancient History
CdE	Chronique d'Égypte
DE	Discussions in Egyptology
GM	Göttinger Miszellen
JARCE	Journal of the American Research Center in Egypt
JEA	Journal of Egyptian Archaeology
MDAIK	Mitteilungen des Deutschen Archäologischen Instituts Abteilung Kairo
NKGWG	Nachrichten, Königliche Gesellschaft der Wissenschaften zu Göttingen (Philologisch-historische Klasse)
PSBA	Proceedings of the Society of Biblical Archaeology
SAK	Studien zur altägyptischen Kultur
ZÄS	Zeitschrift für Ägyptische Sprache und Altertumskunde

1 Aldred, C., "Hairstyles and history," *BMMA* 15 (February, 1957), pp. 141–47. *A study of the Nubian wig, and attribution to Meritaten of the canopic jar stoppers from KV 55*

2 _____ , "The tomb of Akhenaten at Thebes," *JEA* 47 (1961), pp. 41–60. *Proposal that the Tomb 55 occupant is Akhenaten, reinterred with requisitioned funerary equipment along with his mother, Tiye, in a burial from which the queen's body was later removed*

3 _____ , "The Harold Jones collection," *JEA* 48 (1962), pp. 160–62. *Serious doubts cast upon the association with Tomb 55 of most of the fragments published by Bosse-Griffiths in 1961 [15]*

4 _____ , and A.T. Sandison, "The Pharaoh Akhenaten: a problem in Egyptology and pathology," *BHM* 36 (1962), pp. 293–316. *The pathology of Akhenaten, based upon a study of the monuments and anatomical reports on the skeletal remains from Tomb 55; support for Smith's diagnosis of Fröhlich's syndrome*

5 _____ , *Akhenaten, Pharaoh of Egypt—a new study* (London, 1968), pp. 140–62. *The history of the Tomb 55 controversy, and Aldred's revised analysis following Harrison's re-examination of the skeleton, which he finally accepts as that of Smenkhkare*

6 _____ , "Egypt, the Amarna period and the end of the Eighteenth Dynasty," *CAH* II, ch. 19, p. 21. *Tomb 55 and the burial of Smenkhkare in the context of the Amarna period*

7 _____ , *Akhenaten, King of Egypt* (London, 1988), pp. 195–218. *The history of the Tomb 55 controversy, and Aldred's latest views on the deposit: KV 55 a triple reburial from which the mummies of Tiye and Akhenaten have been removed, leaving behind the coffined body of Smenkhkare*

8 Allen, J.P., "Two altered inscriptions of the late Amarna Period, II. 'Son of Akhenaten,'" *JARCE* 25 (1988), pp. 121–26. *Analysis of the foot inscription of the KV 55 coffin, concluding that the alterations had been carried out for a son of Akhenaten rather than for Akhenaten himself*

9 [Anon.], "Discovery of the tomb and mummy of the most famous of Egyptian queens," *The Times* (weekly edition, 15 February, 1907). *Detailed press-report of the Tomb 55 discovery*

10 _____ , "Queen Teie and the heretic King Akh-en-Aten," *The Times*, 3 August, 1907. *The implication of Elliot Smith's identification of the Tomb 55 skeleton as that of a male must be that it is the body of Akhenaten himself*

11 _____ , "American discoveries in Egypt," *National Geographic Magazine* 18 (1907), pp. 801–06. *Contemporary illustrated notice of the KV 55 discovery*

12 Ayrton, E.R., "The tomb of Thyï, *PSBA* 29 (1907), pp. 85–86, 277–81. *The excavator's first accounts of the discovery*

13 _____ , "The tomb of Queen Tîyi," *KMT* 1/2 (summer, 1990), pp. 47–51. *Ayrton's report on the Tomb 55 find, reprinted from Theodore M. Davis, The Tomb of Queen Tîyi (London, 1910), pp. 7–10*

14 Bell, M.R., "An armchair excavation of KV 55," *JARCE* (forthcoming). *Exhaustive survey of the archaeology of Tomb 55*

15 Bosse-Griffiths, K., "Finds from 'The tomb of Queen Tiye' in the Swansea Museum,"*JEA* 47 (1961), pp. 66–70. *Objects formerly in the possession of Harold Jones, mistakenly identified as originating from KV 55; extracts from the Jones correspondence relating to the tomb's clearance*

16 _____ , "Gold-leaf from the shrine of Queen Tiye," *DE* 6 (1986), pp. 7–10. *Analysis of gold leaf said to come from the Tomb 55 shrine*

17 Breasted, C., *Pioneer to the Past. The story of James H. Breasted, archaeologist* (London, 1948), p. 245. *Breasted shown the coffin and bones from KV 55 following their transfer to Cairo*

18 Costa P., "The frontal sinuses of the remains purported to be Akhenaten," *JEA* 64 (1978), pp. 76–79. *Further support for the skeleton's male sex, from measurement of the frontal sinuses; no evidence of the acromegaly postulated by Aldred and Sandison [4]*

19 Cottrell, L., *Queens of the Pharaohs* (London, 1966), pp. 129–52. *Popular account of the Tomb 55 controversy, based upon the articles by Gardiner [28], Fairman [27], Aldred and Sandison [2, 59]*

20 Currelly, C.T., *I Brought the Ages Home* (Toronto, 1956), pp. 141–43. *Brief, eye-witness description of the KV 55 deposit in situ*

21 Daressy, G., "Le cercueil de Khu-n-aten," *BIFAO* 12 (1916), pp. 145–59. *First study of the coffin's inscriptions, and recognition that it had originally been prepared for a woman, perhaps Tiye; subsequent adaptation for Akhenaten; the remains found within perhaps those of Tutankhamun*

22 Derry, D.E., "Report upon the examination of Tut.ankh.Amen's mummy," in H. Carter, *The Tomb of Tut.ankh.Amen*, II (London, 1927), pp. 143–61. *Points of comparison between the mummy of Tutankhamun and the remains from Tomb 55, which are here accepted as those of Akhenaten*

23 _____ , "Note on the skeleton hitherto believed to be that of King Akhenaten," *ASAE* 31 (1931), pp. 115–19. *Reassessment of the Tomb 55 body in the light of Engelbach's attribution of the coffin to Smenkhkare [24]: age about twenty-three, with no evidence of hydrocephalus*

24 Engelbach, R., "The so-called coffin of Akhenaten," *ASAE* 31 (1931), pp. 98–114. *Attribution of the KV 55 coffin to Smenkhkare, based upon a re-examination of its texts*

25 _____ , and D.E. Derry, "The mummy mystery: was it Akhenaten? Hieroglyphic and anatomical evidence," *Egyptian Gazette*, 4 Jan. 1932. *Popular account of the Engelbach-Derry re-attribution of the KV 55 coffin and remains to Smenkhkare*

26 _____ , "Material for a revision of the history of the heresy period of the XVIIIth Dynasty, III. The 'Tomb of Queen Tîyi,'" *ASAE* 40 (1940), pp. 148–52. *Restatement of his 1931 thesis [24], allowing for the possibility that the KV 55 coffin had originally been prepared for a woman*

27 Fairman, H.W., "Once again the so-called coffin of Akhenaten," *JEA* 47 (1961), pp. 25–40. *Proposal that Meritaten was the original owner of the KV 55 coffin, and Smenkhkare its eventual occupant*

28 Gardiner, A., "The so-called Tomb of Queen Tiye," *JEA* 43 (1957), pp. 10–25. *Tomb 55 a reburial of Akhenaten with a miscellaneous selection of surplus funerary equipment; the intended owner of the Tomb 55 coffin, "from first to last," was Akhenaten himself*

29 _____ , Review of Joseph Lindon Smith, *Tombs, Temples and Ancient Art [71]*, in *JEA* 45 (1959), pp. 107–08. *Acceptance of the possibility that the KV 55 coffin had originally been prepared for one of the Amarna princesses*

30 Giles, F.J., *Ikhnaton, Legend and History* (London, 1970), pp. 103–06. *Tomb 55 the hasty burial of Smenkhkare employing surplus funerary equipment*

31 Hanke, R., "Änderungen von Bildern und Inschriften während der Amarna-Zeit," *SAK* 2 (1975), pp. 79–93. *Attribution of the KV 55 coffin to Kiya, whom the author identifies as Nefertiti; the coffin subsequently re-employed for the burial of Smenkhkare*

32 _____ , *Amarna-Reliefs aus Hermopolis* (Hildesheim, 1978), pp. 171–4. *Reconstruction of the KV 55 coffin texts; attribution to Kiya/Nefertiti and subsequent re-employment by Smenkhkare*

33 Harrison, R.G., "An anatomical examination of the pharaonic remains purported to be Akhenaten," *JEA* 52 (1966), pp. 95–119. *Confirmation that that body is male, aged twenty–twenty-five years, and shows no evidence of a delay in maturation; reconstruction of the face by D.J. Kidd*

34 _____ , R.C. Connolly, and A. Abdalla, "Kinship of Smenkhkare and Tutankhamen demonstrated serologically," *Nature* 224 (25 October, 1969), pp. 325–26. *Common blood-grouping of the KV 55 and Tutankhamun remains established as A$_2$MN, strengthening the probability of relationship between the two*

35 Hayes, W.C., *The Scepter of Egypt*, II (New York, 1959), pp. 294–95, 297–98. *An account of those objects from Tomb 55 now in the Metropolitan Museum of Art, New York*

36 Helck, W., "Amarna-Probleme, 4. Der Zeitpunkt des zweiten Begräbnisse des Semenchkare," *CdE* 44 (1969), pp. 212–13. *Dating of the reburial of Smenkhkare within KV 55 to the reign of Horemheb*

37 _____ , "Was geschah in KV 55?," *GM* 60 (1982), pp. 43–46. *Postulates the original presence within KV 55 of a stone sarcophagus which was removed during the reign of Horemheb*

38 Hulin, C., "The history of the Amarna period in Egypt," *Papers for Discussion. Presented by the Department of Egyptology, Hebrew University, Jerusalem* 1 (eds. S. Groll and H. E. Stein, Jerusalem, 1982), pp. 191–209. *Includes a discussion of the identities of Smenkhkare and the mummy from KV 55*

39 Hussien, F., and J.E. Harris, "The skeletal remains from Tomb No. 55," *Fifth International Congress of Egyptology, October 29—November 3, Cairo 1988. Abstracts of Papers* (Cairo, 1988), pp. 140–41. *The Tomb 55 remains those of one person, a male, closely related to Tutankhamun; dentition suggests an age in the middle thirties, anthropological standards and x-rays an age of more than thirty-five years*

40 Ingals, B.K., J.E. Harris, F. Hussien, I. El-Nawawy, N. Iskander, "The skull from Tomb No. 55, Luxor," *Fifth International Congress of Egyptology, October 29—November 3, Cairo 1988. Abstracts of Papers* (Cairo, 1988), p. 142. *Report on the recently (1984) reconstructed skull, and demonstration of its biologic similarity to that of Tutankhamun*

41 Knudsen de Behrensen, Y., "Pour une identification de la momie du tombeau No. 55 de la Vallée des Rois," *GM* 90 (1986), pp. 51–60. *Imaginative reconstruction of the face on the Tomb 55 coffin and support for Kiya's claim to the original and final ownership of it, the canopic jars and the mummy*

42 Krauss, R., "Kija—ursprüngliche Besitzerin der Kanopen aus KV55," *MDAIK* 42 (1986), pp. 67–80. *Study of the KV 55 canopic jars, and confirmation from the text traces that they had originally been prepared for Kiya*

43 Larson, J.A., "Theodore M. Davis and the so-called tomb of Queen Tiye," *KMT* 1/1–1/2 (spring, summer, 1990), pp. 48–53, 60–61; 43–46. *Background to the KV 55 discovery and the personalities involved*

44 Lucas, A., "The canopic vases from the 'Tomb of Queen Tîyi,'" *ASAE* 31 (1931), pp. 120–22. *An examination of the contents of the three Tomb 55 canopic jars now in Cairo*

45 Martin, G.T., "Notes on a canopic jar from Kings' Valley Tomb 55," *Mélanges Gamal Eddin Mokhtar*, II (Cairo, 1985), pp. 111–24. *Proposal, based on text traces on the New York canopic jar, that the Tomb 55 vessels had originally been prepared for Akhenaten; a checklist of the KV 55 material in Cairo and New York; further extracts from the Emma B. Andrews diary*

46 Maspero, G., *Rapports sur la marche du Service des Antiquités de 1899 à 1910*, p. 234. *Preliminary report on the discovery, suggesting the possibility that the occupant of the coffin was a young Amarna prince*

47 _____ , *Essais sur l'Art égyptien* (Paris, n.d.), pp. 147–63 (translated as *Egyptian Art* [London, 1913], pp. 126–34) *The canopic jar lids as portraits of Akhenaten*

48 _____ , *Causeries d'Égypte* (Paris, n.d.), pp. 343–50 (translated as *New Light on Ancient Egypt* [2nd ed., London, 1909], pp. 291–98) *Contemporary account of the discovery by one of the participants: the mummy of Smenkhkare buried as Queen Tiye*

49 _____ , *Guide du visiteur au Musée du Caire* (4th ed., Cairo, 1915), p. 407. *The restoration of the KV 55 coffin*

50 Perepelkin, I.I., *Perevorot Amen-khotpa IV*, I/iii–iv (Moscow, 1967), pp. 114–48. *Incorporates a detailed study of the KV 55 deposit, concluding that the coffin and canopic jars had originally been prepared for Kiya and remodelled for the burial of Akhenaten; the heretic's mummy was later removed from the tomb and replaced with that of Smenkhkare*

51 _____ , *Taina zolotogo groba* (Moscow, 1969) (translated as G. Perepelkin, *The Secret of the Gold Coffin* [Moscow, 1978]). *More popular treatment of the ground covered in Perevorot Amen-khotpa IV*

52 _____ , *Keie i Semnekh-ke-re: k iskhodu solntsepoklonnicheskogo perevorota v Egipte* (Moscow, 1979), pp. 237–57. *Chapter 11: The body from the gold coffin*

53 Reeves, C.N., "A reappraisal of Tomb 55 in the Valley of the Kings," *JEA* 67 (1981), pp. 48–55. *Archaeological analysis of the deposit, which represented a reburial of Tiye and later of Akhenaten within the same chamber, from which the queen's mummy was subsequently removed; reconstructed ground-plan*

54 _____ , "Akhenaten after all?," *GM* 54 (1982), pp. 61–71. *It is argued that the anatomical evidence might be reconciled with the archaeological indications that the skeleton from Tomb 55 is that of Akhenaten*

55 _____ , *Valley of the Kings. The decline of a royal necropolis* (London, 1990), pp. 42–49, 55–60, and passim. *Revised and combined version of the same author's papers of 1981 [53] and 1982 [54]; proposed dating of the final disturbance; first publication of the seals and coffin-band photographs*

56 _____ , *The Complete Tutankhamun* (London, 1990), pp. 20–21. *Brief, popular account of the KV 55 cache*

57 Roeder, G., "Thronfolger und König Smench-ka-Re (Dynastie XVIII), E I–IV. Tod und Bestattung," *ZÄS* 83 (1958), pp. 65–71. *KV 55 the burial of Smenkhkare; the gold-foil patches on the coffin corrections rather than evidence of a change of ownership*

58 Romer, J. *Valley of the Kings* (London, 1981), pp. 211–19. *Popular account of the Tomb 55 discovery*

59 Sandison, A.T., "I. Akhenaten from the monuments" and "II. Skeletal remains found in Valley Tomb no. 55," *JEA* 47 (1961), pp. 60–65. *The pathology of Akhenaten*

60 Sayce, A.H., "The tomb of Queen Teie at Thebes," *The Times*, 17 September, 1907. *Report, following Elliot Smith's male-sexing of the occupant, on Davis's proposal of an ancient mix-up of mummies; Davis's doubts on the validity of Smith's conclusions*

61 Schäfer, H., "Die angeblichen Kanopenbildnisse König Amenophis des IV," *ZÄS* 55 (1919), pp. 43–49. *The canopic jar lids from Tomb 55 as portraits of Nefertiti*

62 Schnabel, D., "Die Rätsel des Grabes No. 55 im 'Tal der Könige,'" *Das Altertum* 22/4 (1976), pp. 226–33. *Popular account of the Tomb 55 enigma, accepting the identification of the body as Smenkhkare*

63 Seele, K.C., 'King Ay and the close of the Amarna age," *JNES* 14 (1955), p. 173, n. 40. *Support for an original female owner for the KV 55 coffin—perhaps Meketaten—in which Smenkhkare was subsequently buried*

64 Sethe, K., "Beiträge zur Geschichte Amenophis' IV, II. Das Lebensalter des Königs," *NKGWG* (1921), pp. 122–30. *The author argues that the estimated age of the Tomb 55 skeleton precludes its identification as Akhenaten*

65 Smith, G. , "The body of Queen Tii," *Nature* 76 (1907), pp. 615–16. *The age and sex of the mummy from KV 55*

66 _____ , "Queen Teie," *The Times*, 15 October 1907. *The age and sex of the occupant of KV 55*

67 _____ , *The Royal Mummies* (Cairo, 1912), pp. 51–56, CG 61075. *The Catalogue général description of the human remains from KV 55*

68 _____ , *Tutankhamen and the Discovery of his Tomb by the late Earl of Carnarvon and Mr. Howard Carter* (London, 1923), pp. 83–91. *Akhenaten diagnosed as perhaps suffering from "Dystocia adiposo-genitalis"—which would explain the apparent delayed maturation of the Tomb 55 occupant*

69 _____ , and W.R. Dawson, *Egyptian Mummies* (London, 1924), pp. 95–97. *Restatement of the possibility that the consolidation of the bones of the KV 55 skeleton was delayed by disease*

70 _____ , "The diversions of an anatomist in Egypt," *Cambridge University Medical Society Magazine* 4 (1926), pp. 34–39. *Includes an account of the controversy over the Tomb 55 remains*

71 Smith, J.L., *Tomb, Temples and Ancient Art* (ed. C.L. Smith, Norman, 1956), pp. 54–75. *Account, based upon contemporary diary entries, of the discovery of Tomb 55 and the subsequent controversy concerning the identity of the skeletal remains*

72 Sotheby Parke Bernet Inc., *Fine Egyptian, Western Asiatic, and Classical Antiquities* sale 3934 (New York, 11 December, 1976), lots 39, 161–64, 253–50. *Sale of pieces formerly in the Theodore M. Davis collection, including elements stolen from the KV 55 deposit and recovered on the Luxor antiquities market*

73 Thomas, E., "The plan of Tomb 55 in the Valley of the Kings," *JEA* 47 (1961), p. 24. *The first published plan of KV 55, not entirely accurate and superseded by the same author's plan of 1966 [74]*

74 _____ , *The Royal Necropoleis of Thebes* (privately printed, Princeton, 1966), pp. 144–46. *1966 assessment of the Tomb 55 deposit; corrected ground-plan*

75 Tyndale, W., *Below the Cataracts* (London, 1907), pp. 184–95. *Contemporary account of a visit to the tomb a week after the discovery*

76 Weigall, A., "A new discovery in Egypt: the recent uncovering of the tomb of Queen Thiy," *The Century Magazine* 74/5 (September, 1907), pp. 727–38. *Popular first account of the discovery by Davis's Antiquities Service inspector*

77 _____ , *The Life and Times of Akhnaton, Pharaoh of Egypt* (Edinburgh and London, 1911), pp. 258–82 (new and revised edition, London, 1922, pp. 228–50). *Popular reconstruction, by Davis's Antiquities Service inspector, of the burial of Akhenaten at el-Amarna; the transfer to Thebes and reburial in Tomb 55 with Queen Tiye; the subsequent removal of Tiye's body and defacement of the coffin and shrine*

78 _____ , *The Treasury of Ancient Egypt* (Edinburgh and London, 1911), pp. 185–208 (later printed as *The Glory of the Pharaohs* [London, 1923], pp. 136–52). *Popular account of the Tomb 55 discovery, identifying the remains as those of Akhenaten reburied in a tomb from which the mummy of Tiye was later removed*

79 _____ , "The mummy of Akhenaton," *JEA* 8 (1922), pp. 193–200 (incorporated in the same author's *The Life and Times of Akhnaton, Pharaoh of Egypt* [new and rev. ed., London, 1922], pp. xiv–xxxi). *A restatement of Weigall's view that the KV 55 occupant is Akhenaten, despite the low estimate of the skeleton's age*

80 Wente, E.F. and J.E. Harris, "Royal mummies of the Eighteenth Dynasty: a biologic and Egyptological approach," in N. Reeves (ed.), *After Tutankhamun: Papers presented at an international conference on the Valley of the Kings, Highclere Castle, 15–17 June, 1990* (London, forthcoming). *Possible re-attributions of the KV 55 skeleton on the basis of craniofacial variation; cites the most recent estimate (by J.E. Harris and F.H. Hussien) of the body's age at death at thirty–thirty-five years*

81 Wilson, J.A., "Mrs Andrews and 'the tomb of Queen Tiyi,'" *Studies in Honor of George R. Hughes* (Chicago, 1976), pp. 273–79. *First publication of extracts from the diary of Emma B. Andrews, Davis's cousin, relating to the KV 55 discovery*

A SKETCH OF QUEEN TÎYI'S LIFE.

BY G. MASPERO.

§ I.—IS THE NEW PLACE THE TOMB OF TÎYI, OR OF KHUNIATONU?

FIRST of all it must be clearly understood that the vault discovered by Davis is not a real tomb; it is a rough cell in the rock, which has been used as a secret burying-place for a member of the family of the so-called Hæretic Kings, when the reaction in favour of Amon triumphed. The transfer of the mummy from its original tomb at Thebes, or El-Amarna, was devised and made in order to save it from the wrath of victorious sectarians; if this had not been the case, it would have been destroyed or robbed of its treasures. Only two Pharaohs are likely to have been actuated by kind feelings for Khuniatonu—those two who were connected with his family, Aî and Tuatankhamanu—it was one of them who planned and executed the operation. That he succeeded in carrying it out secretly is evident from the fact that, while the Tombs of the Kings were desecrated and plundered completely, this place, with its wealth of gold, remained concealed and untouched until last year. The whole furniture was still in it, ready to bear witness as to the name and rank of its owner.

When subsequently tested, its evidence was both obscure and conflicting. Such of the small objects as were inscribed bore the name of Amenôthes III and of his wife Tîyi, proving that the set of tiny pots, boxes, tools, fictitious offerings, in enamelled stone or glazed pottery, were the property of the queen. The big catafalque, in which the body had been borne to its resting-place on the day of the burial, belonged to the same lady, and its inscriptions state that King Khuniatonu ⟨hieroglyphs⟩, " had "made it for the king's mother, great wife of the king, Tîyi." So far, so good, and there seemed to be no possible ground for doubting that the tomb was Tîyi's; but when we came to examine the mosaic coffin and the sheets of gold in which the mummy was wrapped, we found that their legends asserted the mummy to be no other than Khuniatonu himself. It

2

was very badly preserved, having been soaked in water and partly crushed by a block which had fallen from the roof, so that what remained of it was little more than disconnected bones, with a few shreds of dried skin and flesh adhering to or hanging from them. Dr. Elliot Smith, who studied the skull minutely, pronounced it to be the skull of a man aged about twenty-five or twenty-six years. Whether or not he be right about the age is a matter for anatomists only to decide; there is evidence, however, that the body discovered in Davis's vault is that of a man, and that man Khuniatonu, if we must accept the testimony of the inscriptions.

Such being the facts, how are we to reconcile them and explain satisfactorily the presence of Khuniatonu's body amidst Tîyi's furniture? This paradoxical combination may either have been made on purpose, or be the result of some mistake on the part of the persons who executed the transfer. In the first case, we ought, perhaps, to conjecture that, wishing to prevent any harm being done to the king by some fanatical devotee of Amon, the hiders wanted the people to believe that the body they were burying was Tîyi's: accordingly, they took with it Tîyi's catafalque and Tîyi's small furniture, the only exception being the canopic jars which, from the shape of the face, I assume to have been Khuniatonu's. I must confess that I look on this explanation as being too far-fetched to hold good. The second supposition seems to me to be nearer the truth: the mummies of the dead members of Khuniatonu's family must have been taken out of their tombs and brought over to Thebes all together, with such articles of their furniture as it was thought they needed most. Once there, they must have been kept quietly for a few days in some remote chapel of the Necropolis, as were the mummies of Setuî I and other Pharaohs before reaching their last retreat at Deir el-Bahari. When the time came for each to be taken to the hiding-place which had been prepared for them in the Bibân el-Molûk, the men who had charge of these secret funerals mixed the coffins, and put the son where the mother ought to have been. Visitors to the Cairo Museum, who have seen the coffins of Iouîya and Touîyou, and how like they are to each other, will not wonder at such a confusion having been made, especially if we suppose that the transfer took place at night time.

I believe that Davis's vault was originally designed for Tîyi, and for Tîyi's furniture, but that Khuniatonu's mummy was buried in it by mistake. There is still some chance that Khuniatonu's appointed tomb may be discovered in the Bibân el-Molûk with Tîyi's mummy lying in state amongst her son's property

§ II.—THE FACTS ABOUT TÎYI.

The name ⟨hieroglyphs⟩ is read sometimes Thïy : even if it were proved that the sign ⟨hieroglyph⟩ was pronounced commonly *th* in the language of the second Theban Empire, the syllabic ⟨hieroglyph⟩ has for its equivalent ⟨hieroglyphs⟩ with a ⟨hieroglyph⟩ *t*, and not a ⟨hieroglyph⟩. The pronunciation Tîyi, or with the dialectal E, Têye, is the right one, and is supported by the testimony of the Assyrian monuments.

Tîyi was a daughter of Iouîya and Touîyou, his wife, both of whom were Egyptians of mediocre, if not of low, extraction.[1] Iouîya seems to have been originally a member of the priesthood of Minu, lord of Akhmîm, a prophet of that god ⟨hieroglyphs⟩, and a superintendent of his herds of oxen ⟨hieroglyphs⟩. Touîyou was a "Chauntress of Amanu" ⟨hieroglyphs⟩ "and a tire-woman of the king" ⟨hieroglyphs⟩, not, as it has been said, "the "Mistress of the robes," but one of the women who kept the robes of the king in order, and who helped to dress him every day. The higher titles and epithets, which we find affixed to their names on their own coffins and funerary furniture, were given to them in after life, when their daughter was queen of Egypt.

There are a few dated monuments of Tîyi's life, scarabs for the most part. Perhaps the most important of them is that one which records the Wild Cattle Hunt, not so much on account of the facts on it, but because it has a date of the second year of Amenôthes's reign :—

⟨hieroglyphic inscription⟩

"The IInd year, under the Majesty of King Amenôthes III, and the Great "Wife of the King, Tîyi, living like Raîya."[2]

---

[1] See Davis, *The Tomb of Iouîya and Touîyou,* pp. xiii–xxiv.

[2] Two specimens of these scarabs are known : the first belonged to Mr. G. W. Frazer, and was published by him in the *Proceedings,* t. XXI, Pl. III, pp. 155, 156, and in the *Catalogue* of his collection of scarabs, Pl. XVI and p. 56 ; the second belonged to the Rev. W. MacGregor, and was published by Newberry, *Scarabs,* Pl. XXXIII, 1, and pp. 173–176.

The form of the date proves that the indication of the second year applies as much to her as to her husband, as she was already a queen at that early date. After this second year, there are no dated monuments of her until we come to the tenth year, and then two scarabs were issued, one recording the number of lions which the king had killed with his own hand :—

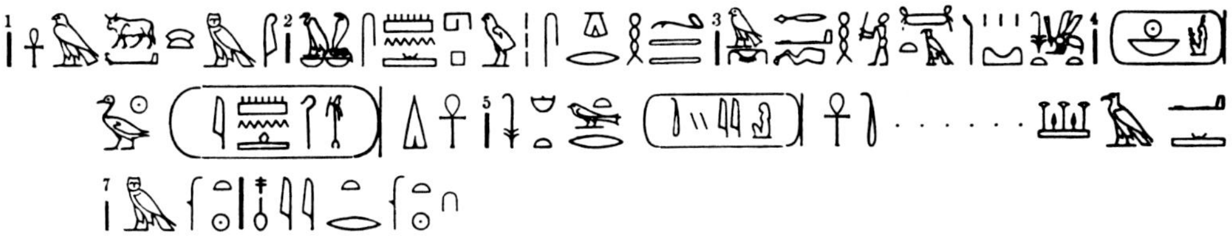

[hieroglyphic text]

"King Amenôthes III and Queen Tîyi, living . . . from the first year until
 "the year 10 . ."[1]

while the second refers to the coming to Egypt of Giloukhipa, daughter of Shoutarna, king of Mitani :—

[hieroglyphic text]

"Year 10, under the Majesty of King Amenôthes III and Queen Tîyi, living,
 "whose father's name is Ioûîya, and whose mother's name is Touîyou."

The last date in the combined reign of Amenôthes and Tîyi is that of the eleventh year, and is to be found on a scarab which relates the inauguration of an artificial lake in the city of Zaloukha :—[3]

[hieroglyphic text]

---

[1] About forty specimens of this scarab are known, for an account of which I refer to Newberry, *Scarabs*, Pl. XXXII, 2, and p. 171.

[2] Two copies of it are known, one in the Berlin Museum, the other in the possession of Baroness Hoffmann ; *cf.* Newberry, *Scarabs*, Pl. XXXII, 1, and p. 170.

[3] This name, which had been correctly read by the first Egyptologists up to the time of Wiedemann (*Aegyptische Geschichte*, p. 382), was miscorrected into Zalou-Selle of the Delta; the true reading has been restored lately by Steindorff and Breasted (*Zeitschrift*, 1901, pp. 62-66).

"Year 11, third month of Akhaît, the first, under the Majesty of King
  "Amenôthes III and Queen Tîyi, living.—His Majesty ordered a lake
  "to be made for Queen Tîyi, living, in her town of Zaloukha, 3,700
  "cubits in length, 700 cubits in breadth. His Majesty made the
  "[usual] feast for the opening of the lakes, in the third month of
  "Akhaît, the sixteenth, when His Majesty sailed upon it in the royal
  "barge *Atontahunu*."

The town of Zaloukha is otherwise unknown, but Steindorff, Breasted,
and Newberry all came independently to the conclusion that it was identical
with the palace-town of Amenôthes III and Tîyi, which was discovered by
Grébaut and partly excavated by Tytus six years ago : the lake which the
king made for his wife would be the modern Birket Habou. Even conceding
that the so-called Birket Habou is the site of an old reservoir—which has
never been proved—the difference between its dimensions and the measurements on the scarab is so great, that it is difficult to admit the proposed
identification.

From this eleventh year to the end of the reign we possess no dated record
of Tîyi but one document, and this, though bearing no mention of a regnal
year, refers to an event which happened, at the latest, in the first year. This
is the so-called Marriage scarab : [2]

"King Amenôthes III and Queen Tîyi, living, whose father's name is Iouîya
  "and whose mother's name is Touîyou, and who is the wife of the
  "strong king, whose southern boundary is to Kalaï, and the northern is
  "to Naharaina." [3]

  [1] With reference to the four specimens of this scarab which are known, *cf.* Newberry, *Scarabs*,
Pl. XXXIII, 2, and pp. 176–178.
  [2] Newberry, *Scarabs*, Pl. XXXII, 3, and p. 172.
  [3] Breasted, *Antient Records of Egypt*, t. II, pp. 344, 345, and *A History of Egypt*, pp. 329, 330.

The conclusion that this scarab was issued in remembrance of the marriage has been drawn from the insistence with which Amenôthes says that "the "Great Wife of the king, Tiyi .... she is the wife of the strong king." It seems to me, however, that the real meaning of the inscription is to be elicited, not from that part of the inscription, but from the last words, in which the limits of the empire are indicated: they assert the power of Amenôthes and the extent of his dominions in such a way, that they lead us to suppose that the scarab was destined to proclaim the accession of a new king. I should therefore see in it an Accession, and not a Marriage, scarab. The reason why the king put so much stress on the fact that Tiyi was his wife, is probably to be sought for in the departure from traditional customs which he made when he inserted her name in the official protocol: no queen had been thus honoured before his time. If this interpretation prevailed, it would confirm us in the opinion that Amenôthes married Tiyi while he was still heir to the crown.[1]

Those are all the dated facts in the united lives of Amenôthes III and Tiyi; the undated are not so scarce, and they bear witness to the powerful influence which Tiyi exerted on her husband. She acted with him in the ceremonies for the consecration of the temples he restored or built. Thus, at Soleb, in Nubia, where Amenôthes was associated with the cult of Amon-ra, she followed him with her sons and daughters, and she made homage to his deity;[2] to show his gratitude, he built a temple for her, at Sedeinga, of which temple she was the Goddess.[3] In Egypt itself she appears next to him on the famous Memnon Colossi at Thebes, and on numerous small objects, lists of which are to be found in recent books on the history of Egypt;[4] we learn from them nothing more than what we knew already from other sources. The only monument which is of interest for us is the large group from Medinet Habu, now transferred to the Cairo Museum:[5] there we see her sitting next to her husband, and with them three of their daughters:

[hieroglyphs] Nabîtâhâou, [hieroglyphs]

[hieroglyphs] Honîttannebu, and a third one, whose

[1] Breasted, *A History of Egypt*, p. 329, admits the possibility of his having married Tiyi "already as crown prince."

[2] Cailliaud, *Voyage à Méroé*, Atlas, t. II, Pl. 14; Lepsius, *Denkmäler*, III, Pl. 83–88.

[3] Lepsius, *Denkmäler*, III, Pl. 82, e-i.

[4] Wiedemann, *Aegyptische Geschichte*, pp. 389-392; Flinders Petrie, *A History of Egypt*, t. II, pp. 202, 203.

[5] Daressy, *Notes et Remarques*, § CCII, in *Recueil de Travaux*, t. XXIV, pp. 165, 166.

name has completely disappeared. Honîttaunebu is probably identical with the 𓀀𓄿𓎺𓎛𓏏, who, according to Lepsius, was represented in the temple at Soleb.[1] The group is in the best Theban style of the period, with idealized features: the face of the queen is rounded and regular, and bears very little resemblance to her real face as it is known to us from the head found by Petrie in Sinai.

Tîyi bore many children to Amenôthes III, only five of whom are known to us, four daughters, 𓇳𓎺𓏏𓁐 Isît,[2] 𓎺𓄿𓁐 Honîttaunebu, transcribed in error 𓀀𓄿𓎺𓏏𓁐 Honitmerhabi,[3] 𓊃𓈗𓃒𓏏 Sîtamanu who was probably the third daughter in the group in the Cairo Museum,[4] 𓃒𓈗𓏏𓏏 Bakîtniatonu, of whom more anon, and a son who was afterwards the celebrated Amenôthes V—Khuniatonu. Nothing but the name is known concerning the three eldest daughters, and the place of the fourth in the family was misunderstood until quite recently. As she appears only at El-Amarna, and bears a name composed with Atonu, she was supposed to be a daughter of Khuniatonu. Now we have proof that she was Tîyi's daughter, born, probably, somewhat late in the reign of Amenôthes III.[5] The original form of her name may have been 𓃒𓈗𓏏𓈗 Bakîtniamanu, and the final Amanu changed to Atonu during her brother's reign; this, however, is mere conjecture. She must have been quite young when her father died, for she is represented as a girl in the twelfth year of Khuniatonu, and was unmarried at that time. As none of the three eldest sisters are alluded to under Khuniatonu, it seems probable that they died in their father's lifetime.

When her son came to power, Tîyi continued at first to enjoy great authority. The king of Mitani, Dushratta, wrote directly to her and implored her to exert her influence with her son, to obtain for him certain favours, or according to his view rights, he was claiming, and whenever he

[1] Lepsius, *Denkmäler*, III, Pl. 86*b*; *cf.* Lepsius, *Königsbuch*, no. 379, and Bouriant-Brugsch, *Le Livre des Rois*, no. 356.

[2] Lepsius, *Denkmäler*, III, Pl. 86*b*; *cf.* Brugsch-Bouriant, *Le Livre des Rois*, no. 356.

[3] Flinders Petrie, *Illahun*, Pl. XVII, no. 20; Daressy, *Notes et Remarques*, § CCII, in *Recueil de Travaux*, t. XXIV, pp. 165, 166 and under the faulty form, Lepsius, *Denkmäler*, III, Pl. 86*b*.

[4] Birch, in *Archaeological Journal*, t. VIII, p. 297; Mariette, *Abydos*, t. II, Pl. 49; Flinders Petrie, *Tell el-Amarna*, Pl. XIII, no. 16; Dr. DAVIS, *The Tomb of Iouîya*, pp. 38, 43.

[5] Flinders Petrie. *A History of Egypt*, t. II, pp. 203, 204; N. de G. Davis, *The Rock Tombs of El-Amarna*, t. III, Pl. XVIII, and pp. 15, 16.

wrote to Khuniatonu, he adjured him to consult his mother about the friendly relations he had entertained with her husband. [1] Nevertheless, it seems that after a time she was, if not put completely aside, at least left out of most political affairs. She is never mentioned in the documents in which Khuniatonu narrates how he founded his new capital and inaugurated or enlarged it; only his wife, Nofrîteîti, and her daughters are represented as participating with the king in the rites of consecration. Is this a sufficient reason to allow us to affirm that, though she had a palace in El-Amarna [2] and a household, of which a certain Houîya was a superintendent, [3] she did not reside there habitually, but that she lived, most of her time, in her palace at Thebes? It needs more proofs than we have to make such an assertion, and to draw from it the conclusion that, far from being the inspirer of the Atonian creed, she preferred to keep out of it as far as it was compatible with her dignity of mother of the reformer. One thing only is certain, that is, that about the twelfth year of her son's reign ⟨hieroglyphs⟩, [4] she was in El-Amarna. I say *about* the twelfth year, because the date relates, not to any fact in which she was necessarily concerned, but to a reception by the king of Syrian and Ethiopian tributes, and Tîyi's visit might have occurred somewhat earlier or somewhat later. The different episodes of her stay are depicted freely in Houîya's tomb. A tableau is dedicated to the memory of her husband, and associates him with the honours she is receiving from her son. Amenôthes III sits on a chair in front of his royal wife, and raises his own hand towards one of the small hands with which the rays of the sun are provided. Her protocol is written behind her :

" The Princess, the most praised, the lady of grace, sweet in her love, who fills
    " the palace with her beauties, the Regent of the South and the North,
    " the great wife of the king who loves him, the lady of both lands, Tîyi,"

exactly as if her husband was still living. In front of her, her youngest daughter, Bakîtatonu , raises her hand

    [1] Winckler, *Die Thontafeln von Tell el-Amarna*, pp. 68–81.
    [2] Flinders Petrie, *Tell-Amarna*, Pl. XXII, and p. 33.
    [3] See his titles in N. de G. Davis, *The Rock Tombs of El-Amarna*, t. III, Pl. I–XXV, and pp. 1–25.
    [4] N. de G. Davies, *The Rock Tombs of El-Amarna*, t. III, Pl. XIII, p. 9.

towards her father.[1] In another place we see how she was invited to the table of the king, and how she sat in front of her son and of her daughter-in-law with Bakîtatonu ; she is crowned with the diadem of the two feathers and the sun-disk on flaming horns, while Pharaoh and his wife wear an ordinary head-dress.[2] The entertainment was protracted till late into the night, and ended in a kind of drinking bout,[3] as in some of the tales in the *Arabian Nights*. Further on, it is shown how she was led by her son to the temple of Atonu,[4] where a part of the building was known as the *Sun-shade of Tîyi*, in parallelism with the *Sun-shade* ⸢⸣ of her son.[5]

Thus she disappears from our eyes in a kind of apotheosis.

§ III.—CONCLUSION.

When we come to examine coolly the few facts which are known about Tîyi, very little remains of the romance with which most early writers have surrounded her person. She was an Egyptian, born of parents of low, or, at the best, of middle condition, and her father was in the service of a provincial Egyptian god. She was already married to Amenôthes when he notified officially his accession to the throne, and she was invested by her husband with the full honours of a reigning queen of Egypt. Her fame passed the frontiers of Egypt, and the vassal or allied kings of Asia tried to win her goodwill whenever they were in need of help, or when they claimed a gift from their liege. Her power lasted till the death of Amenôthes III and continued for awhile under Amenôthes IV, but she probably remained in Thebes and came to Khuniatonu occasionally ; her last visit was about the twelfth year of her son's reign. It seems probable that she died in his lifetime. Whether she was buried at Thebes or at El-Amarna, we are not able to say. I have already given above, in Section I of this sketch, a possible explanation of the facts connected with the presence of part of her funerary apparel in the hiding place at Bibân el-Molûk.

MILON-LA-CHAPELLE,
22nd September, 1908.

---

[1] N. de G. Davies, *The Rock Tombs of El-Amarna*, t. III, Pl. XVIII, and pp. 15, 16.
[2] *Ibid.*, t. III, Pl. IV, V, and pp. 4–7.
[3] *Ibid.*, t. III, Pl. VI, VII, and p. 7.
[4] *Ibid.*, t. III, Pl. VII–XII, and pp. 7–9.
[5] On this *Sunshade*, cf. N. de G. Davies, *The Rock Tombs of El-Amarna*, t. III, pp. 19–25.

A NOTE ON THE ESTIMATE OF THE AGE ATTAINED BY THE PERSON WHOSE SKELETON WAS FOUND IN THE TOMB.

BY

G. ELLIOT SMITH, M.A., M.D., F.R.S.,

*Professor of Anatomy in the Egyptian Government School of Medicine, Cairo:
sometime Fellow of St. John's College, Cambridge.*

WHEN these bones were sent to me for examination two years ago, I reported that they formed the greater part of the skeleton of a young man, who, judged by the ordinary European standards of ossification, must have attained an age of about twenty-five or twenty-six years at the time of his death. At the same time I called attention to the fact that the dates at which the various bones of the human skeleton underwent consolidation and ceased growing were subject to a very wide range of variation in different individuals, so that a bone which had reached its full development in one person at twenty years of age might, in another, be still incomplete at twenty-five, and a vertebra, which might be complete at twenty-five years of age in one man, may take five years longer to become consolidated in another person.

Such considerations led me to make the reservation that the estimated age of twenty-five or twenty-six years might, in any given individual, be lessened or increased by two or three years, if his growth was precocious or delayed, respectively. The question has been put to me by archaeologists: " Is it possible that these bones can be those of a man of twenty-eight or thirty years of age? " For the reasons indicated above, no anatomist would be justified in denying that this individual may have been twenty-eight, but it is highly improbable that he could have attained thirty years if he had been normal.

The cranium, however, exhibits in an unmistakable manner the distortion characteristic of a condition of hydrocephalus. The bones, therefore, cannot be regarded as those of a perfectly normal person, so that there is the possibility—though it is nothing more—that the process of ossification may not have followed the usual course, but have been delayed.

To make this position clear would need a somewhat detailed examination of the technical evidence, which Mr. Davis tells me he does not want for the purposes of this volume.

All that I need state here at present is that, taking the evidence of such standard authorities as POIRIER (PAUL POIRIER ET A. CHARPY, *Traité d'Anatomie Humaine*," Tome I^{ier}, 1899) and TESTUT (*Traité d'Anatomie Humaine*," 1899), and examining it in the light of the data regarding the relation of the times of consolidation of various bones, the one to the other, in a large series of ancient Egyptian skeletons, I still maintain the opinion mentioned above :—that the skeleton is that of a man of twenty-five or twenty-six years of age, without excluding the possibility that he may have been several years older.

GRAFTON ELLIOT SMITH.

THE FINDING OF THE TOMB OF QUEEN TÎYI.

THEODORE M. DAVIS.

ON the 1st of January, 1907, having exhausted the surrounding sites, I had to face a space of about forty feet oblong and at least fifty feet high, covered with limestone chippings, evidently the dumping of the surrounding tombs. Within a few feet was the open tomb of Rameses IX, and on the east and south sides were the open tombs of Seti I, and Rameses I, II, and III ; all of which had contributed to the hill. There was no sign of the probability of a tomb. On the contrary, it seemed to be a hopeless excavation, resulting in a waste of time and money. Nevertheless, it had to be cleared, whatever the result. Possibly it may interest the reader to know that the most difficult, delaying, and expensive work is the finding of a place where the débris can be dumped. Generally, it has to be moved two or three times, as the first dumping-ground may probably cover some tomb, therefore the débris must be returned to the original spot, in case no tomb is found.

With a large gang of men, we commenced clearing on the apex of the hill, within a few feet of the tomb of Rameses IX. In the course of a few days we reached the level of the door of his tomb, finding nothing but the chippings of the surrounding tombs. But down we went some thirty feet, when we found stone steps evidently leading to a tomb. Finally, we discovered the lintel of a door which proved to be about eight feet high and six feet wide. It had been closed with large and small stones, held in place with cement or plaster, but, with the exception of a wall about three feet high, these had been pulled down. The clearing of the door, so that we could enter, was soon done, when we found that within a few feet of the door, the mouth of the tomb was filled with stones to within four feet of the roof. On this pile of stones were lying two wooden doors, on each of which copper hinges were fixed. The upper faces of the doors were covered with gold foil marked with the *name and titles of Queen Tîyi*. It is quite

13

impossible to describe the surprise and joy of finding the tomb of the great queen and her household gods, which for these 3,000 years had never been discovered.

The next and most difficult task was to pass the " doors," as they filled the space between the walls and could not be moved for fear of injuring the gold inscriptions. However, with the skill of the native captain, we got a beam about ten inches wide between one wall and the golden door. On this beam I managed to crawl over, striking my head and most of my body but without damaging the doors. I then made my way down the tomb, finding some stones and sand. En route, we noticed many small objects. Within seventy feet we came to a break in the corridor about six feet deep, which proved to be a room about fifteen by eighteen feet, whose walls and roof had been badly cemented. To the right, some five feet from the floor, was a cutting in the rock, about four feet square and three feet high, and in it were four canopic jars with the heads on ; these bore no hieroglyphs and no signs of the original owner.

On the floor near by lay the coffin made of wood, but entirely covered with gold foil and inlaid with semi-precious stones, as will be seen from the photograph in the catalogue. Evidently the coffin had either been dropped or had fallen from some height, for the side had burst, exposing the head and neck of the mummy. On the head plainly appeared a gold crown, encircling the head, as doubtless it was worn in life by a probable queen. Presently we cleared the mummy from the coffin, and found that it was a smallish person, with a delicate head and hands. The mouth was partly open, showing a perfect set of upper and lower teeth. The body was enclosed in mummy-cloth of fine texture, but all of the cloth covering the body was of a very dark colour. Naturally it ought to be a much brighter colour. Rather suspecting injury from the evident dampness, I gently touched one of the front teeth (3,000 years old), and alas! it fell into dust, thereby showing that the mummy could not be preserved. We then cleared the entire mummy, and found that from the clasped hands to the feet, the body was covered with pure gold sheets, called gold foil, but nearly all so thick that when taken in the hands, they would stand alone without bending. These sheets covered the body from side to side. When we had taken off the gold on the front of the mummy, we lifted it so as to get the gold underneath, which was plainly in sight. Mr. Joseph Lindon Smith, an artist drawing for me, put his hands under a large sheet of gold, and, as he lifted it up, exclaimed: " I have something on my hands which you have never found before." When he gave it to me, I put my hands under it and found them wet with water.

It may be interesting to know how the water got into the tomb and why it remained there. There was a narrow crack in the rock roof within ten feet of the door of the tomb, which I noticed had been originally cemented, evidently as protection against the rain. There was very near it a crack not wider than a knitting-needle, extending six or eight feet. Doubtless, it was supposed that no water could get in there, but it proved not to be so. Probably for many years the water had percolated through the crack and had run down the steep stone floor to the chamber where the mummy lay on the ground. It must be understood that the tomb was absolutely airless, except for what was originally shut in, and what possibly came through the "needle" crack, which after some years was hermetically closed by the dumpings from the numerous surrounding tombs. The air had absorbed all the dampness that it could from the objects in the tomb, but had not the power to absorb the water underneath the body. (In the Iouîya and Touîyou tomb I found a large open alabaster jar, two-thirds full of liquid, probably natron.)

We then took off the gold crown, and attempted to remove the mummy-cloth in which the body was wrapped, but the moment I attempted to lift a bit of the wrapping, it came off in a black mass, exposing the ribs. We then found a beautiful necklace, which is now in the Cairo Museum. It was around the neck and resting on the breast beneath the mummy-cloth.

Subsequently the wrappings of the mummy were entirely removed, exposing the bones. Thereupon, I concluded to have them examined and reported upon by two surgeons who happened to be in the "Valley of the Kings." They kindly made the examination and reported that the pelvis was evidently that of a woman. Therefore, everyone interested in the question accepted the sex, and supposed that the body was doubtless that of Queen Tîyi. Some time thereafter, the bones were sent to Dr. G. Elliot Smith, Professor of Anatomy in the Egyptian Government School of Medicine, Cairo, for his inspection and decision. Alas! Dr. Smith declared the sex to be male. It is only fair to state that the surgeons were deceived by the abnormal pelvis and the conditions of the examination.

Within a few feet of the coffin, the four alabaster canopic jars were standing in a small excavation in the stone wall. The heads were on the jars, but, on examination, it proved that the ordinary contents had been removed before the jars had been deposited in the tomb. There had been inscriptions on each vase, but for some unknown reason they had been carefully obliterated, but the "sky" sign clearly shows on every jar.

There have been some suggestions that the heads are portraits of Khuniatonu (Amenhotep IV). It seems to me to be certain that if the heads were his, they would have been extremely elongated as was his usual practice. In evidence of this, it will be seen on a plaque which Khuniatonu caused to be made of wood, covered with gold foil, whereon is Tîyi's portrait, he represented her head and face elongated in his usual style (see Plates 29–33). From these and other evidences, I venture to insist that the beautiful canopic heads are portraits of Queen Tîyi.

There were many very interesting objects in the tomb which I have not mentioned, but by reference to the admirable catalogue of objects made by M. George Daressy, the reader can understand the interest of the find.

In all probability her mummy was buried in a tomb in Tell el-Amarna, and probably would have remained there, but owing to the danger of the destruction of her body during the disturbances after the death of her son, Tut-ank-Amon, the son-in-law of Khuniatonu, doubtless brought the mummy and all the objects theretofore described, and took possession of the tomb. This we know because I found in the tomb several lead seals with his name recorded. No one seems to know why the contents of the tomb were not stolen or destroyed when they reached the tomb in the Valley; nor can one understand why the gold crown at least was not taken by the priests or the workmen.

The tomb in which Tîyi's objects were found was not excavated for her, as M. Maspero says, nevertheless it was not disturbed until I found it. It seems reasonable to suppose that it was so insignificant that it was allowed to remain undisturbed. In addition to this, the makers of the surrounding tombs treated the site as a barren place to dump the rocks from the various tombs, thereby protecting Tîyi's deposit. We all know that insignificance spares many people from various troubles, as was the case with Tîyi and with Iouîya and Touîyou.

A short time ago, I found a small pit tomb about three hundred feet from Tîyi's tomb. It was covered with rock and sand about three feet deep. It proved to be about seven feet square and six feet deep. It was filled with white jars sealed with covers. We opened them and found that one contained various interesting objects pertaining to burials. The remainder of the jars contained small red cups, many square limestone blocks, fairly well polished, and many other objects of little value, etc. Evidently they came from a poor man's tomb, from which the contents were carefully removed and secreted in the pit tomb I have described. In all probability the contents were removed for the purpose of finding a tomb for Queen Tiyi. The poverty of the style of the tomb suggests that it was the only one that could be found in the vicinity. In any event, it seems that the selection of this tomb probably protected the deposits from robbery.

I have recently found in one of the jars a bundle of mummy-cloth which had been used for the protection of some of the fragile objects. On spreading it there appeared hieroglyphics reading, "Good God, lord of Egypt, loved by Min. Year 6th." It therefore is certain that he directed the clearing of the tomb of all its contents, which he deposited in the Pit-tomb, and then took possession of the tomb wherein he deposited all the objects of Queen Tîyi.

THE EXCAVATION OF THE TOMB OF QUEEN TÎYI, 1907.

EDWARD R. AYRTON.

THE central point and the meeting place of all the Wadis at the southern end of the Valley of the Tombs of the Kings at Thebes is occupied by a large rock mound, in which Rameses IX excavated a great tomb for himself, running into the western face ; and various smaller tombs have been discovered to the north of his sepulchre on the western and northern sides of the mound. The western face to the south of the tomb was, however, covered with an immense heap of limestone chips thrown out by the masons engaged in cutting the tomb of Rameses VI which lies opposite, and, as this had never been touched in more recent times, we removed the greater part in the hopes of finding some older tomb of importance beneath.   After sinking deep pits and trenches down the side of the rock face, we had almost given up hope when we came across several large jars of the XXth dynasty type lying together in what appeared to be a recess in the rock.   On digging deeper we came to a cut face with squared corners on either side, showing that a tomb had at least been begun at this spot.   We then sunk a pit straight down through the chippings, which at this depth were cemented together by the action of water, until we came to a layer of clean dry limestone fragments which led us to hope that the tomb might have escaped the fate of that of Siphtah which we had found so damaged by the entrance of water.   Below this clean rubbish we struck a flight of well-cut stone steps and knew that we had discovered a tomb of the XVIIIth dynasty and no mere burial pit.

Turning on our full gang of men we made a thorough clearance down to the entrance of the tomb, which had evidently been begun on a smaller scale and then enlarged.   We found the doorway closed by a loosely-built wall of limestone fragments, resting not on the rock beneath, but on the loose rubbish which had filled the stairway. This we removed and found behind it the remains of the original sealing of the door. This was composed of rough blocks of limestone cemented together and coated on the outside with cement of so hard a quality that a knife could scarcely scratch it ; on this we found the impressions of the oval seal of the priestly college of Amon-ra at Thebes— a jackal crouching over nine captives. This wall we also removed and began the clearance of the corridor, which we found filled with rubbish to within some three feet of the ceiling, near the first doorway, and sloping towards the other end until the space from the ceiling was almost six feet. This rubbish consisted of clean limestone chippings which gave the appearance of never having been moved far from the tomb or left outside for any length of time. Lying on this rubbish, at a few feet from the door by which we had entered, lay a large wooden object resembling a broad sled in shape. It was covered with gold-leaf with a line of inscription running down each side. On it lay a wooden door with copper pivots still in place ; this also was covered with gold-leaf and ornamented with a scene in low relief of a queen worshipping the Sun-disk. On both of the objects lay fragments of limestone which had injured the gold. When we examined the gold we discovered the cartouche of the famous Queen Tiyi. Our workmen succeeded in improvising a bridge consisting of a narrow beam without injury to the gold. We crawled along this narrow bridge and over the rubbish beyond we came to a second doorway which was more or less clear of rubbish. From the sill we clambered down a long broad slope of chippings and débris into a large oblong room, the walls of which were coated with stucco, but undecorated. The interior seemed to be in a state of complete confusion. On the slope down which we had just come lay a wooden door exactly similar to that which we had found in the corridor, and beside it stood a large alabaster vase-stand. Against the opposite wall of the room were leaning what appeared to be the sides and cornice of an enormous casket-shaped box. On the ground to the left lay another side of apparently the same box, whilst square beams lay scattered about the floor. Wherever the woodwork lay horizontally the stucco and gold-leaf still adhered and the scenes and inscriptions on them were consequently preserved ; but of the pieces leaning against the wall, only one still retained part of its original decoration. In the further corners lay the remains of small wooden boxes, and in a small chamber or recess in the right-hand wall one could distinguish the four canopic jars. Just beneath the recess there lay a wooden coffin covered with gold-leaf and inlaid with carnelian and glass; it had fallen in on one side exposing the head of the mummy, on which appeared a gold crown.

All the woodwork in the tomb was, however, in so fragile a state that nothing could be touched and it was therefore decided that, besides the usual views of the interior, photographs should be taken of each thing as it stood before we attempted the removal of anything. An expert photographer was telegraphed for from Cairo, and work on the tomb was suspended for a few days until he had taken the desired photographs, since we found that the shifting of rubbish so stirred up the dust as to quite obscure all outline, and would therefore be fatal to photography. The photographing finished, we began the clearance of the corridor. On first entering we had noticed, at a few feet from the door, a long crack in the roof, which had been ineffectually stopped up with cement, through which a certain amount of rain-water had entered the tomb, and it was owing to this accident that the woodwork in the large room was so fragile. The water had had the same effect on the wood in the corridor, and we found that it would be quite impossible to remove it without damaging the designs on the surface. We therefore decided to leave it in position, and this we were able to do by careful underpinning of the whole structure with planks and beams, which enabled us to remove the whole of the rubbish from beneath, leaving it suspended in air.

In the rubbish of the corridor, which we now removed as far as the entrance of the room, were only found a copper graving tool, a wooden mallet head, and a few beads, whilst we found that the old woodwork had been partly upheld at one end by the lid of what must have been a very large alabaster vase. We now had sufficient space to work in and turned our attention to the coffin. The lid had, as we have already noticed, collapsed inwards, splitting into two halves from the feet to the neck; we were consequently able to remove it in three sections, laying each piece as it was removed on a specially prepared padded tray, and each in turn was then carried out and placed in the corridor.

Beneath this lay the remains of the mummy, wrapped in flexible gold plates, but the wrappings had been so affected by moisture that they crumbled to the touch, and the bones would only just bear handling.

Round the neck were the remains of a broad necklace of gold pendants and inlaid plaques connected by rows of minute beads, and ending in large lotus flowers of gold, inlaid with paste. The left arm was bent with the hand on the breast, and round the upper arm were three broad bracelets of very thin gold of a fragile nature; the right arm was laid straight down by the side, the hand resting on the thigh, and remains of three similar bracelets were round the wrist; no rings or other jewellery were found with the mummy.

Under the coffin was a long wooden boarding covered with gold-leaf, at the head of which were found lions' heads in wood, suggesting that the coffin had originally lain on a raised couch, which by collapsing, had let the coffin fall to the ground, and the falling lid had thus broken up the mummy.

After we had moved the canopic jars from the small side-chamber, we started sifting the whole of the rubbish on the floor, and were rewarded by finding numerous small objects.

In the south-west corner were the remains of a large oblong wooden box, which had collapsed under the weight of stucco fallen from the wall above. The wood was, however, in good condition, and we were able to remove it. Between this and the west wall were the remains of another box of small size—which may have originally fitted into the larger—so affected by the moisture that it crumbled to the touch. It had been full of small vases, wands, and figures of blue glazed ware.

Four inscribed mud tablets, on two of which the cartouche of Akhenaten is legible, were found, respectively (a) in the north-west corner; (b) under the mummy couch; (c) in the small side-chamber; and (d) against the east wall at about seven feet from the north-east corner.

In the rubbish under the funeral couch and behind the boards against the south wall we found numerous fragments of small clay seals, some of which bore, besides the device, the cartouche of Neb-kheperu-ra (Tutankhamen). The remains of a necklace of small blue beads were found near to the north-east corner scattered about in the rubbish.

CATALOGUE OF THE OBJECTS

FOUND IN THE

TOMB OF QUEEN TÎYI,

BY

GEORGE DARESSY.

I. SEPULCHRAL CANOPY.

1. The Sepulchral Canopy.—The entrance corridor and the sepulchral chamber contained the panels of a great sarcophagus, or, more precisely, of a hearse which must have served to protect the coffin during its transport to the necropolis. The catafalque, of rectangular form, which opened in front with folding-doors, is made of cedar-wood, now rotted by damp; it was covered with stucco, engraved and gilded, but this decoration also is in bad condition and is breaking off in fragments to such an extent that there is no hope of preserving it. Copies made on the spot by Mr. Ayrton enable me to give the following details:

Front. On the upper traverse two inscriptions face each other; left, [hieroglyphs]; right, [hieroglyphs]. (Pl. XXXV.)

DOOR-POSTS.—On the posts forming the jambs of the door is a vertical column of hieroglyphs, and the ornament [hieroglyph] at the base. On the left jamb was inscribed[1] [hieroglyphs]

[hieroglyphs]

[1] As there is no typographical sign in existence representing the [sign] under the Aten disc, the sign ♀ has been substituted therefor.

[hieroglyphs]. The prenomen of Amenôthes IV had been erased and that of Amenôthes III substituted in red ink.

On the right-hand post: [hieroglyphs] [hieroglyphs]. (Pl. XXXV.)

DOOR.—One of the leaves of the door was found in the corridor; the other in the chamber. The bronze hinges were still attached to them (see No. 3).

On them Queen Tïyi was figured offering flowers to Aten, the rayed disc. The legends engraved above this scene referred, some of them, to the disc: [hieroglyphs] [hieroglyphs] (below 1 and 2)

[hieroglyphs], others to the Queen, [hieroglyphs]

Back.—Inscription of the upper border twice repeated symmetrically:

[hieroglyphs]

On the left upright: [hieroglyphs];
on the right: [hieroglyphs].

The panel is entirely occupied by a scene of adoration of Aten. (Pl. XXX.) The disc placed near the left corner emits rays terminating in hands; some of these receive the offerings, and others protect the king and queen, holding the sign of life to their nostrils. The altar placed below the disc bears six cartouches, those of Aten, twice repeated, and those of the king, which have been erased. Besides what is placed on the altar, there are tables laden with bread and food-products, and amphorae are placed in light wooden stands. The king, the whole of whose figure has been erased, was standing about the middle of the scene, wearing on his head the helmet with two striped ribbons, and holding the baton ⑂ employed to strike objects offered to divinities. Behind him is Queen Tïyi dressed in a long airy robe; her neck covered with a wide necklace, her head adorned by a wig of small curls; her forehead is encircled by a crown, in front of which are two uraei with the horns of Isis on their heads; she is wearing the headdress of the goddess Hathor, the disc surmounted by two long feathers. The features of the queen are remarkable : she has the long face and prominent chin that characterise the portraits of the reign of Khuniatonu. She seems to be pouring water on the pile of offerings in front of her, out of which flames are apparently issuing. (Pl. XXXIV.)

Inscriptions are engraved above this scene, referring to the disc :

or to the king and his mother :

LARGE PANELS.—The stucco of the lateral panels is in a worse condition than that of the ends. It is only possible to recognise that the scenes on them also are adoration of the rayed disc and the dedication of altars of offerings. (Pl. XXXI.) The horizontal inscription above the scene reads thus :

2. **Bronze Tenons.**—Four bronze tenons found among the rubbish served to fasten the cover to the sarcophagus described above. They are roughly rectangular in form, with rounded corners, strips of metal, 6 to 7 millimetres in thickness. Their dimensions, length and breadth, are : A.—0 m ·23 × 0 m ·068 ; B.—0 m ·21 × 0 m ·065 ; C.—0 m ·23 × 0 m ·07 ; D.—0 m ·225 × 0 m ·07. The upper part of the second tenon has been completely severed. It was cut in a straight line through half the thickness of the metal by chisels, and then snapped off by wrenching it sideways. (Pl. XXV.)

The upper half of the tenons were inserted into the wood of the cover, and fixed there by a bronze peg 0 m ·038 in length : the lower half to a depth of 0 m ·115 fitted into a cavity worked in the thickness of the sarcophagus. On each tenon there is a column of inscription bearing the name and title of Queen Tïyi :

3. Door Hinges.—The folding-doors of the catafalque still retained their two bronze hinges, length 0 m ·13, heights with the pivots 0 m ·25 and 0 m ·09. They consist, as usual, of one piece, hollow and rectangular, that fitted round the edge of the door; its breadth is 0 m ·045, the space between the sides being 0 m ·04 : to this is attached a conical pivot in the case of the lower hinge, the upper one has a cylindrical pin. These objects seem to have been covered with gold-leaf, now fallen off as the result of oxydation. On the lintel of the door there was still the hollow bronze cylinder, height 0 m ·04, diameter 0 m ·048, in which the upper hinge of the door revolved.

II. COFFIN.

4. Coffin.—The coffin that contained the mummy is the richest and most highly decorated of all that have hitherto been found. Sculptured, gilded, and inlaid, the completion of the various processes employed in its ornamentation must have occupied a considerable length of time. Unfortunately, it has reached us in a very bad state of preservation, the boards disjointed, the wood rotted, the stucco powdering off, and the inlays falling out of their sockets, the result of so many centuries spent in a tomb into which water had penetrated.

The coffin is in cedar-wood, of human form, and consists of two pieces, the receptacle and the cover, held to each other by tenons. Its length is 1 m ·75, its breadth 0 m ·56. The whole represented the king at full length, wrapped in bandages from which emerged the head and the two hands crossed on the breast. There is no part which was not either gilded or inlaid with stones and enamel. (Pl. XXXII.)

The face was covered with a gold mask, of moderate thickness. Of this the lower part is missing from below the eyes, which were inlaid ; to the chin was attached a false beard (see no. 6). The head was covered with a wig similar to that on the heads of the canopic vases (see Pl. IX.): the hair is carefully divided into small coils, parted at the top of the head and falling vertically all round, except in front where they are caught back to the sides of the face in five rows laid over each other, each row diminishing in length. At the back they leave the neck uncovered, but they lengthen by degrees, till in front the two points touch the breast. This hair is carved on pieces of ebony inserted in the wood of the coffin, and thinly covered with gold-leaf. On the forehead is a uraeus in bronze gilt, with the body trailed over the head (see no. 5).

The arms are laid on the breast; the crossed hands are closed and hold the royal emblems, the crozier and whip (see no. 7); on the wrists are wide bracelets adorned with plaques of multicoloured glass. For the remainder of the surface, the wooden case was covered with a coating of fine plaster, over which gold-leaf was laid more or less thickly; but following a traced design the gilding was cut away, the plaster hollowed and the cavities filled with cut stones or with coloured glass moulded to the shape of the cavities to be filled. These inlays were fixed by a blue or green mastic. For this decoration—polychrome upon a gold ground—the effect of which is very good, the artists employed carnelian for the red, glass coloured with metallic salts for the lapis-blue, turquoise-blue and emerald-green, crystal or crystallised gypsum for the white.

The upper part of the breast is concealed by a collar 16 centimetres wide, composed of seven rows of different ornaments arranged in the following order:

1st row.—Inverted semicircles, red, ▽, interspaced with triangles, green, △.

2nd row.—Tongues, white, ⋃.

3rd row.—Disc in relief, gilded except at the top, a segment inlaid, green, ⊖. These alternate with small chess-boards, ten squares in length by five in height. Here gold squares separate others which are successively blue, red, blue, green, blue in the first row. In the lower rows the colours are repeated in the same order, but each time moving on one colour towards the left.

4th row.—Inverted semi-circles, ▽, separated by triangular petals cut in three pieces, △, the top pale blue, the centre red, the base lapis-blue.

5th row.—Pendant flowers, blue, with a red point projecting from the centre of the corolla, ⨇, between them are elongated green triangles, in imitation of folded leaves, ⌒.

6th row.—Small semi-circles, ▽, between which hang blue glass triangles, striped down the length, △.

7th row.—Pendant flowers, composed of a green calyx above, and a spreading corolla below in striated blue glass, △.

The rest of the body is ornamented in accordance with the method of decoration customary at the commencement of the XVIIIth dynasty, and which has caused the Arabs to give to these coffins the name "rishi," or "feathered." But, while the sarcophagi of Amasis, Nefert-ari, and of the Thothmes' have feathers that cover the entire surface, simply engraved on a thin coating of plaster, which was afterwards gilded, here the feathers are inlaid in a variety of colours, and the gold only marks the outlines.

All the feathers point in the direction of the feet ; those that cover the bust are small with rounded ends, and are imbricated—height 3 centimetres, width 15 millimetres. Each is formed of three pieces, the top lapis blue, the middle a chevron of turquoise-blue, the base red.

The lower part of the body is decorated according to a different scheme. Down the middle there is an inscription which extends from the arms to the feet. The hieroglyphs, of polychrome inlays, stand out on a plain gold ground, 0 m ·065 wide. On each side of this there are twelve long vertical rows, 2 centimetres wide, in imitation of quills, formed by small plaques of glass arranged in chevrons, successively blue, green, blue, red. The whole of the surface at this level is filled with this scheme of colour.

The column of hieroglyphs between the legs gives the royal titles of Khuniatonu :

On the sides, horizontal bands of inscriptions follow the junction of the coffin and its cover. They repeat the same titles, with one sole variant at the commencement :

The end of the coffin at the foot is covered with gold leaf, on which twelve lines of hieroglyphs are finely engraved, seven upon the cover, five upon the coffin :—

[Six lines of hieroglyphs]

The interior of the coffin was also covered with gold leaf, averaging from 0 m ·42 to 0 m ·20. Down the middle both of the coffin and of the lid there is a single column of hieroglyphs, which were engraved in the wood, and the gold pressed down over it to receive the imprint. These merely give the royal protocol once more, with unimportant variants in the orthography : [hieroglyphs] (coffin [hieroglyphs]) [hieroglyphs] [hieroglyphs] (coffin [hieroglyphs]) [hieroglyphs] (coffin [hieroglyphs]), followed on the cover by [hieroglyphs] [hieroglyphs].

The cartouches of the king have been everywhere destroyed, but the epithet "living for the Truth" is entirely peculiar to Khuniatonu.

5. **Uraeus.**—On the coffin, over the forehead, a uraeus was fixed, emblem of the light that the sovereign, even as the sun, was reputed to shed around him. (Pl. IV, Fig. 5.) The snake is in solid bronze; height 85 millimetres. The greatest thickness of the neck is 4 centimetres. The top of the head is gilded, as well as two vertical cartouches and a series of sixteen narrow scales above which they are placed in the axis of the neck, and also six plaques arranged symmetrically on the sides. The cartouches contain the name of the rayed disc :—

[Two cartouches with hieroglyphs]

6. **Beard.**—The beard, length 0 m ·13, which was affixed to the chin, is of wood, gilt and inlaid with blue and green enamel plaques, arranged in diagonals, chevestred to represent the false plaits that the Egyptian

kings, always clean shaven, wore on their chins during certain religious ceremonies.

7. Flagellum.—In the closed hands must have been placed the crozier and whip, emblems of the royalty of Osiris, god of the dead, with whom all the dead were assimilated. The crozier and the handle of the whip, which, doubtless, were of gilded wood, have disappeared; all that remain are the three thongs of the whip. They are three bronze rods, length 0 m ·23; on each of them were threaded at least eight small hollow pieces of dark blue glass, in the form of truncated cones, increasing in size from the top to the bottom, and separated from each other by as many pieces of the same shape in gilded wood, almost all of which are destroyed. (Pl. VIII, Fig. 3.)

III. ORNAMENTS OF THE MUMMY.

8. Crown.—The head of the mummy was covered by way of a crown, with thick gold foil carved in the shape of a vulture. (Pl. XXII.) The length from back to front is 24 centimetres, its breadth 21 centimetres. The body of the bird is straight to the front, the head turned to the right; each foot (the left one is broken) held a ring Ω, emblem of long duration. The wings, instead of being extended horizontally, are raised in a semicircle, so much so that the tips overlap each other, and two rings placed on the outer edge of the wings are superimposed. The whole is of slightly conical form, fitting well to the head; the empty space between the wings measures 0 m ·115 in width. The lower edges are bent back, and thus form a rim a millimetre in width to consolidate the crown. On the left wing an ancient repair can be seen: the gold foil having been accidentally pierced, the damage was repaired by means of a piece of the same metal soldered below the puncture.

The whole surface is delicately engraved: the details of the head and feet, all the feathers of the body, and the wings with their quills are indicated by lines in repoussé. This piece, unique of its kind, is a magnificent specimen of the goldsmith's art of the XVIIIth dynasty.

9. Necklace.—It has been possible to reconstruct the necklace reproduced on Plate XXIII from the gold beads and plaques found in the coffin. The breadth is 0 m ·32, the height 0 m ·565. The details are as follows : Two little bars, each surmounted by a lotus flower formed the ends of the necklace ; these bars are in gold, length 0 m ·09, and form a tube, not soldered, almost square in section, and pierced with six holes for the strings on which the beads were threaded. Upon the tube, at the opposite side to the holes, and occupying only half the length, a triangular piece of gold is attached with a ring at the top to which is fastened a lotus flower in cloisonné ; the calyx is gold, the central petal and those at the sides are lapis-lazuli, the intermediate petals are gold. The remainder of the space is filled with two pieces : one of green glass in the angle ; the other, that which formed the rounded end, was probably of red enamel, but all the plaques are missing.

This necklace consists of five rows of ornaments : the first of these is formed of eighteen plaques of cloisonné on gold, the whole of which is in imitation of the plaited garlands of leaves and flowers with which mummies were surrounded. Each plaque has a tongue-shaped ornament, in three colours : the top is gold, from the centre piece all the inlay has fallen out, but it was probably in carnelian, the lower part has lapis-blue glass. To the left of this ornament a piece of turquoise-blue enamel is fitted, which increases in size at the base in such a way as to fill in the space between the leaves. Four small gold beads are attached to the plaque, two above, two below, through which it was threaded ; beads in blue, green, and red glaze, threaded on the upper string between the attachments of these plaques form, with them, a continuous row of beads. (Pl. XXIII.)

The remainder of the necklace consists of hollow gold beads, flat behind, and with a small ring at each end. Of these there are forty-three in the form of a flower-bud $\langle\rangle$, 21 centimetres in length ; sixteen of the same kind only 17 to 19 centimetres ; fifty-one semi-cylindrical, with rounded ends $\bigcap$, 21 centimetres in length ; and, finally, thirty-four of the same dimensions shaped like flower petals $\bigwedge$.

10. Necklace Ornaments.—Small gold and inlaid plaque analogous to those in the first row of the preceding necklace, measuring 18 millimetres in length and 15 in height. The scheme of decoration is twice repeated. It comprises a folded leaf pointed at the tip. The basis is a semi-circle in gold, the remainder being worked in lapis-blue glass ; at the side a small gold leaf contains a model of a flower, of which the calyx is in gold, the corolla carnelian and lapis-blue glass. The empty space between them is filled with turquoise-blue glass ; all the inlays are set into gold cloisons and fixed with blue mastic. The back of the plaque is marked ₁₁₁^₁₁₁₁, probably to indicate that the piece was the seventeenth of the row. Two gold beads attached to the upper part, and two others at the base kept the ornament in place between two threads.

11. **Necklace Ornament,** hollow, in form of the royal cartouche; vertical, with a ring at top and two at the base ; height 0 m ·02, width 0 m ·007. On one of the faces the name of the solar divinity is inscribed in hieroglyphs, stamped in hollow relief ⚲ ꙮ ⚱ ⚲ ⚳ .

12. **Flower, gold and inlaid.**—Piece of jewellery, height 0 m ·035, width 0 m ·027, in the form of the flower symbolic of Upper Egypt (Pl. VII., Fig. 7.) The lower part is a plain gold plaque, the gold calyx is in three striated divisions ; the corolla, inlaid with lapis-blue glass, is separated into two parts ending in volutes, whose centres are open. Between these two petals there is a third with rounded top, forming the highest part of the flower, represented by a plaque of carnelian. At both ends a small ring is attached.

13. **Beads.**—Three cylindrical beads, which have been recovered in frag-ments ; may have belonged to the same piece of jewellery, necklace, or bracelet. The first is in red glass, length 0 m ·023, diameter 0 m ·012 ; it was covered with gold leaf. The hole is almost square.

The second in lapis lazuli, length 0 m ·022, diameter 0 m ·011, has also a square hole.

Of the third, in green felspar, only one end remains, length 0 m ·018, and 0 m ·01 in diameter, with a round hole 4 millimetres.

Other beads of various shapes and materials have been found, but it is impossible to discover whether they belong to necklaces other than the preceding. There are flowers, ☙, and ⌂, some *dad*, 𝔶, in carnelian, lapis, and light-blue glass. Two other kinds of beads in blue glass must have formed a network laid over the body. One of these has the appearance of an elongated olive pierced with four holes, the others are cylindrical, lined in spirals, bevelled at one end to allow of their being strung together in **V** form.

14. **Fasteners for Earstuds.**—The earstuds have not been found, the back parts only remain. These are two gold nails, 32 millimetres in length, the head rounded at the top, flat below, 7 millimetres in diameter, and a stem with a blunt end. The ear ornament must have been in gold and circular in form, having at the back a tube to go through the ear. The heads of these nails, pushed into the tubes, would serve as guards and keep them from falling out.

15. **Piece of Gold Foil, engraved.**—A thick piece of gold foil, 0 m ·018 in height, 0 m ·016 in breadth, which was probably attached to some material. On it are stamped in relief the two cartouches enclosing the names of Aten :

placed together vertically. The shape of the plaque follows the outlines of the two cartouches.

IV. CANOPIC VASES.

SERIES of four canopic vases in alabaster. The embalmed intestines that they contained have perished, and all that now remain are the bituminous rags with which they were padded. (Pls. IX to XXI.)

16. **The Vases,** of the ordinary form of this class of object, are 0 m ·368 in height, 0 m ·155 diameter at top, 0 m ·24 at the largest part, and 0 m ·16 at the base. The diameter of the opening is 0 m ·114, and the depth of the cavity inside 0 m ·34.

The exterior was decorated with a scene, apparently a representation of some personage in adoration before a divinity, but it has been obliterated with such care, that, beyond the outlines of the sign ⊙, no group of the inscriptions is now visible; the sky ⊨, at the top of the picture, was so deeply engraved that it was not possible to erase it, and it has been filled in with pieces of alabaster polished down to the level of the adjacent parts of the vase.

The human heads, which form the covers of the vases, are carved out of magnificent transparent whitish alabaster; height 0 m ·08, of which 0 m ·018 millimetres form the rim that fits into the vase. The diameter at the base is 0 m ·16, and the internal cavity 0 m ·12.

The type is that of a woman, and recalls the portraits of Queen Tiyi, wife of Amenôthes III, more especially the fine head in soapstone found by Mr. Flinders Petrie in Sinai. The finest of the four heads, which is also the best preserved, has the same elongated face, with the lower part somewhat prominent, and pointed and rather hanging chin, as in the representations of Khu-n-aten, though less pronounced; the nose is straight and rather shorter than in the three other examples; the cheeks are full; the eyes, which are long, but not widely opened, are inlaid, the circumference is in blue enamel, the cornea in white limestone, with the corners painted red, the iris in black jasper; the brows, also in blue enamel, are highly arched. The four faces present almost the same characteristics; in the other three the chin is slightly less elongated, and the face rather broader, making altogether a rounder countenance. The head-dress is a wig, the line of the cap showing on the forehead. Short behind, where it leaves the neck uncovered, it gradually lengthens, and ends in two points touching the clavicles, falling straight down the sides of the face, which it encloses, hiding the ears. It is divided into a number of small coils that fall vertically from the top of the head, except in front where the hair is cut short, and forms three rows on the forehead and on the sides of the face, where the locks are arranged obliquely, and end in an arrangement of five rows, diminishing in length one above another.

On the forehead is a uraeus in alabaster, made of a separate piece fitted into the cover. On all the vases this is broken off close to the surface and only the tail remains stretched out over the head as far as the occiput.

The lower part of the cover broadens out and covers the top

of the vase; it is decorated as if it were the breast, with a necklace of three rows of cylindrical beads arranged vertically, and a row of piriform beads. The ornament [ ] behind serves as fastening and counterweight.

The inscription on the vases having been erased, we do not know to whom this series of canopics belonged. At that period both men and women wore this kind of wig, but the features being feminine and the face beardless, while the heads bear the royal uraeus on the forehead, it may be presumed that these vases were made for a queen, and, in all probability, for Queen Tiyi, wife of Amenôthes III, and mother of Khuniatonu.

V. RELIGIOUS OBJECTS AND AMULETS.

17. Socle of a Statue.—Socle in cedar wood; length 0 m ·21, breadth 0 m ·138, depth 0 m ·065. It is an unornamented block, with a hollow on the top, 0 m ·09 in length and 0 m ·07 in breadth. The shape shows that it fitted a statue in form of a human mummy, Osiris, Ptah, or a funerary figure.

18. Figurine of Thot.—A small plaque; height 0 m ·056, length 0 m ·038, thickness 0 m ·006, in greenish glazed pottery, cut out in the shape of the god Thot, a crouching figure turning to the right. The object was broken in two, and the end of the ibis beak is missing. A ring for suspension is placed behind the head.

19. Magical Bricks.—A chapter of the Book of the Dead—the 151st according to M. Naville, the 137th according to Mr. Wallis Budge— prescribes that bricks of unbaked clay, mixed with incense shall be placed in the tomb, towards the four cardinal points. On them were to be fixed various objects, and they should bear certain magical texts. The tomb has yielded the series of four bricks, with the name of Khuniatonu, in more or less good condition, but made on two models.

19a. Northern Brick.—Length 0 m ·18, breadth 0 m ·10, depth 0 m ·045. It is complete with the exception of a fragment from one end. (Pl. XXIV.) It is of Nile mud, sun-dried, the surface washed over with fine greyish clay, lighter than that of which the brick is made. On the top five horizontal rows of hieroglyphs—the ritual text—have been traced in black and then engraved :—

Behind this text there can be seen the hollow which held the foot of a wooden statuette, similar to one found in the tomb of Touiya (p. 29, Pl. 22), and in front the hole left by a peg.

19b. Southern Brick.—Length 0 m ·205, breadth 0 m ·095, thickness 0 m ·04. It is almost intact (Pl. XXIV.), and is made like the preceding brick. It is inscribed with seven lines of hieroglyphs :—

The end of the first line is covered with a mass of bituminous substance, and the whole of the top of the brick has been soaked with some liquid. In the centre of the space between the beginning of the text and the end of the brick, a twig can be seen inserted in the brick, which has been burnt to charcoal. It is, therefore, quite possible that a small piece of wood was soaked with bitumen and then burnt. I am disposed to believe that after the funeral ceremony, this torch was replaced by a dummy lamp. In the tomb was found an object shaped like a truncated cone, height 0 m ·04, measuring 0 m ·065 in diameter at the top, and 0 m ·03 at the bottom, in green glazed pottery. It had a hole in the middle at the top. (Pl. V, Fig. 1.) This may have been a model of a vase used as a lamp, the flame represented by a twig, which is now destroyed, which would be placed on the brick in order to conform with the prescribed ritual.

19c. Western Brick.—Length 0 m ·09, breadth 0 m ·095, thickness 0 m ·03.

The two last bricks are less thick than the first, and they are also in bad condition. On the brick of the west there are five lines of hieratic, traced lengthways; the left half of this object, on which a dad 𓊽 should be placed, has perished. The text transcribes thus :—

19d. Eastern Brick.—Only a fragment of this remains 0 m ·11 × 0 m ·09, thickness 0 m ·026, with only a few hieratic signs of the text

FOUNDATION DEPOSITS.

It is only a very small part of the votive objects commemorating the construction of the tomb that was deposited in this hiding place. The pieces belonging to this category are :—

20. Four small Alabaster Bricks, polished on all the faces except underneath; uninscribed. Their length varies from 0 m ·106 to 0 m ·108, the breadth from 0 m ·031 to 0 m ·032, and the depth from 0 m ·014 to 0 m ·016. (Pl. IV, Fig. 7.)

21. Two Pieces of Red Jasper.—The first of these, 0 m ·055 long and 0 m ·025 wide, is of oval section and appears to be a pebble, showing no signs of working. The second, 0 m ·065 long and 0 m ·022 wide, is of lenticular section, and the edges, without being sharp, are everywhere regularly fined off. (Pl. VII, Figs. 9 and 10.)

22. Four Alabaster Discs, the edges bevelled, or rounded below, the top being flat in all cases. Their diameter varies from 0 m ·023 to 0 m ·03, and their depth from 0 m ·004 to 0 m ·006.

23. Libation Vases.—Three small libation vases of somewhat rare type, in green glazed pottery, discoloured, 0 m ·11 to 0 m ·128 in height, and 0 m ·059 to 0 m ·066 in breadth. (Pl. VI, Fig. 5.) Here the ordinary libation vase is combined with the emblem of life ☥. The vase, without its foot, takes the place of the handle of the emblem *ankh*, which it almost resembles in form, although the neck at the top modifies the outline.

24. Uza (Sacred Eye).—The Uza, 𓂀 or eye of the sun, the amulet which above all others kept every misfortune at a distance, is represented by a certain number of examples in greenish glazed pottery, that may be classed in seven groups. They were moulded; some have merely a ring for suspension; others are in no way pierced, and cannot have been threaded for wear.

First type.—Fifteen examples, length 0 m ·025. The eye is engraved on both sides of the plaque. The white of the eye and the space between the eye and the supporting coil are cut out in open work. The eyebrow is engraved with angulated lines ⟨.

Second type.—Four examples, length 0 m ·035. The eye is only engraved on one side, as is the case with those described subsequently. Here they turn to the right 𓂀; the lower part is open work. (Pl. V, Fig, 4.)

Third type.—One example only, length 0 m ·035. It is a pendant to the preceding; the eye turned to the left.

Fourth type.—Six examples, length 0 m ·025. Eyes turned to the right, the lower part carved.

Fifth type.—Six examples, length 0 m ·025. Eyes forming pendants to the preceding turned to the left.

Sixth type.—Three examples, length 0 m ·025. Eyes similar to those of the fourth type, but without the space between the eye and its support.

Seventh type.—Five examples. Eyes making pendants with the preceding, turned to the left, and not in open work.

25. Papyrus Stems.—The amulet *uaz* 𓌀, which represents the stem of a papyrus, terminating in its flower, assured to the deceased perpetual verdure. Three models of these have been found.

First type.—Two examples, length 0 m ·14 and 0 m ·15. The stem is slender (the largest diameter is 2 centimetres) and flattened. The glaze is bright green, to conform with the regulations laid down in Chapters 159 and 160 of the Book of the Dead, which directs that this amulet shall be made in green felspar.

Second type.—Two pieces, similar but smaller. Length 0 m ·083 and 0 m ·081 ; the stem is round and thin ; diameter 0 m ·013.

Third type.—The eight last examples are more massive, and the green glaze is discoloured. Their length varies from 0 m ·08 to 0 m ·09 ; the medium size of the stem, whether round or slightly flattened, is 0 m ·023. (Pl. IV, Fig. 6.)

26. The Mooring Pole.—Amulet in glazed pottery, height 0 m ·165, maximum breadth 0 m ·019 ; represents a post for mooring a boat. (Pl. VII, Fig. 5.) The upper part, for 0 m ·04 of its length, is cylindrical. Then comes an abrupt lateral projection, which continues down the length, diminishing in width, giving the object rather the appearance of the blade of a knife. One of the promises made to the deceased was that he should sail in the barque of the Sun ; this post is one of the objects intended for the outfit of the divine mariners.

27. Models of Papyrus.—Sixteen cylinders in glazed pottery, representing rolls of papyrus supplied to the deceased to enable him to read the prayers and incantations required by him. (Pl. IV, Fig. 8; Pl. VII, Fig 1.) The cylinder has a longitudinal line marking the end of the roll, and, with the exception of the two first examples, a spiral engraved at the ends indicates the coils of the papyrus. These cylinders have been moulded in pairs ; their length is not proportionate to their size.

Their dimensions are as follows :—

2 rolls of 0 m ·10 in length, 0 m ·014 in diameter.
2 „ 0 m ·088 „ 0 m ·017 „
2 „ 0 m ·081 „ 0 m ·022 „
2 „ 0 m ·08 „ 0 m ·018 „
2 „ 0 m ·075 „ 0 m ·02 „
2 „ 0 m ·073 „ 0 m ·02 „
2 „ 0 m ·064 „ 0 m ·012 „
2 „ 0 m ·057 „ 0 m ·015 „

28. Serpents' Heads.—Three heads of the uraeus serpent, in blue glazed pottery ; these probably formed the ends of magical sticks, the wooden handles of which have perished.

The first measures 0 m ·03 in length, 0 m ·019 in breadth. The eyes are inlaid with carnelian; at the top of the head there is a square hole for fixing a headdress (disc?) that no longer exists.

The second, length 0 m ·027, breadth 0 m ·019, has only one eye in carnelian set in gold. A thin stem of bronze passes through the head.

The third, length 0 m ·03, breadth 0 m ·019, still has both eyes in carnelian, but one of the behind extremities is broken. There is no hole in the head.

29. **Two small Plaques** of greyish schist cut in the shape of the amulet Pesesh-kef, which appears to have possessed the virtue of endowing the mummy with power to use the orifices of the body. It is often confused with the headdress *Ten* ⟩⟨, formed of two ostrich feathers.

The first is 0 m ·13 in height, 0 m ·056 in width at the top, and 0 m ·045 at the base, 0 m ·009 in depth. It is made of two pieces fastened together and arranged thus : .

A column of hieroglyphs on the left side of one of the two faces is this inscription of Queen Tïyi :

The other plaque, 0 m ·138 in height, 0 m ·073 in breadth at the top, 0 m ·058 at the base, and 0 m ·01 in thickness, bears no inscription.

VI. VARIOUS OBJECTS.

30. **Casket.**—Casket in wood with rectangular panels : the cover is in form of a double-pitched roof. The panels are of cedar wood, painted outside in red, framed with strips of black ebony veneer, 0 m ·032 wide. The length is 0 m ·57, the breadth 0 m ·43, the box is 0 m ·27 in height, and with its feet 0 m ·30 ; the elevation of the cover is 0 m ·09. At each end of the panels there are three slender tenons, fitting into the upright pieces at the corners. These last have perished, but the slips of ebony that covered them remain.

The cover is of the same work ; the panels and the triangular pinions are framed with ebony. At the top, near one end of the ridge, a square hole marks the position of a knob.

On one of the sloping sides of the cover, there is a hieratic inscription written in black ink, which transcribes thus : "That which is in gold of the household vases." This casket therefore contained pieces of gold plate which have not been discovered.

31. Fragment of a Piece of Furniture.—Fragment 0 m ·12 in height, 0 m ·08 in width, part of a piece of furniture. The wood of which it was made was falling into powder and so decomposed that it could only be preserved by covering it with a coating of wax. The cartouche of Queen Tiyi is engraved on it, beside the prenomen of her husband Amenôthes III.

32. Casket in glazed pottery.—Casket in green glazed pottery, discoloured, 0 m ·08, breadth 0 m ·055, height 0 m ·039, and with a cover 0 m ·046, made on the model of wooden boxes. It is supported on four feet; the panels are rectangular, with projecting frames, and surmounted by the Egyptian cornice. (Pl. VI, Fig. 4.)

The cover has a slight pitch, sloping towards the back, with an abrupt drop of a quarter of a circle in front; two small cross pieces are fixed to the under side; one in front, of square section, merely served to hold the cover in place when closed; the other at the back, of this section ⫞, is fitted into a groove in the panel of the box and forms a pivot for the cover.

Two knobs were fixed on the front, one on the lid, the other on the box, and served both as handles and to fasten the casket when it was desired to close it effectually, by tying strings to the knobs and sealing them.

33. Five Caskets in glazed pottery.—The green colour has either faded or turned brown. Simpler in make than the former they have rectangular panels resting on two cross pieces placed at the ends. (Pl. V.) The covers are flat, and have on the lower side two cross pieces, one plain the other bevelled, of varying forms, corresponding with a hollow or projection in the inner side of the back panel of the box.

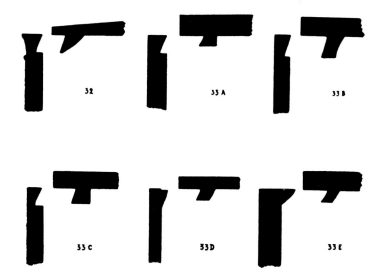

The characteristic features of these five caskets are as follow :—

	Length.	Breadth.	Height.	Height with the Cover.
A.	0 m ·08	0 m ·057	0 m ·047	0 m ·054
B.	0 m ·08	0 m ·051	0 m ·043	0 m ·049
C.	0 m ·078	0 m ·048	0 m ·04	—
D.	0 m ·075	0 m ·044	0 m ·039	—
E.	0 m ·073	0 m ·046	0 m ·035	0 m ·04

All the caskets, except the fourth, have two knobs, one of which is on the cover.

34. Vases in glazed pottery.—The most numerous objects of this find are small cups in the form of truncated cones. They are in green glazed pottery ; in some instances the colour has turned almost white, in others a yellowish brown. It is the shape of vase used for holding fruit, and for drinking cups, as well as for lamps, in which case a wick was burnt in the oil. There are twenty-four cups of this class, more or less high in comparison with their diameter. The largest is 0 m ·073 in diameter at the top, 0 m ·033 at the base, and 0 m ·04 in height ;

the smallest 0 m ·045 and 0 m ·024 in diameter and 0 m ·032 in height. The others are of various sizes, the medium dimensions being, height 0 m ·032 and diameter 0 m ·052 and 0 m ·026. (Pl. VI, Fig. 2.)

35. Five small Vases in glazed pottery in the shape of water-jars. (Pl. II, Fig. 6.) The mouth is wide, the contraction for the neck is very slight, the base rounded. Their dimensions are as follows :—

	Height.	Diameter at top.	Maximum Diameter.
A.	0 m ·07	0 m ·029	0 m ·038
B.	0 m ·07	0 m ·027	0 m ·037
C.	0 m ·07	0 m ·027	0 m ·035
D.	0 m ·067	0 m ·03	0 m ·036
E.	0 m ·067	0 m ·25	0 m ·033

It can be seen that the vases have been moulded in two halves, and joined in the baking.

36. Two similar Vases, but the necks are cylindrical and the bases flat.

	Height.	Diameter at top.	Maximum Diameter.
A.	0 m ·08	0 m ·025	0 m ·035
B.	0 m ·08	0 m ·024	0 m ·034

37. Vase, 0 m ·059 in height, 0 m ·028 and 0 m ·038 in diameter at the mouth and the belly, similar to one of the preceding vases without the neck.

38. Two other Vases in greenish glazed pottery, 0 m ·067 in height, 0 m ·024 diameter at the top, and 0 m ·030 diameter at the widest part. The base is pointed and they have no necks, but they diminish steadily in size from the top downwards.

39. Vase Stands.—The preceding vases required stands to keep them upright. Fifteen of these supports have been found in discoloured green glazed pottery : they are rings of rectangular section more or less high in proportion to their size. (Pl. V, Fig. 6.) They can be classified into four different types :—

		Height.	External Diameter.	Internal Diameter.
7	stand	0 m ·008	0 m ·035	0 m ·029
2	,,	0 m ·007	0 m ·033	0 m ·027
3	,,	0 m ·012	0 m ·031	0 m ·024
3	,,	0 m ·012	0 m ·029	0 m ·022

40. Toilet Jar.—One of the most interesting pieces in this find is **one in** green glazed pottery, now almost white : a statuette of a woman carrying a jar on her shoulder. (Pl. III, Fig. 2.) The total height is 0 m ·077. The socle being 0 m ·026 and the figure alone 0 m ·054 in **height,** The rectangular socle, 0 m ·036 by 0 m ·023, was made **separately,** and has two holes in which the feet of the woman were fixed. The vase is spherical and has a wide, straight neck with a slight brim, and a rounded handle on the side. The woman carrying it on her left shoulder is supporting it beneath with both hands, and to restore equilibrium is bending the upper part of her body sharply to the right. This slave is dressed in a long garment without ornamentation ; her hair, which is reddish-black, falls freely round her head on to her shoulders, framing her face. The design is charming, and it is to be regretted that the artist who modelled this piece did not treat it with greater delicacy and more detailed ornamentation.

41. Haematite Vase.—Small toilet jar in black haematite, 0 m ·058 in height, 0 m ·037 diameter at the top, 0 m ·046 in the middle, 0 m ·03 at the base. (Pl. VI, Fig. 3.) The interior is almost similar to the exterior in shape. It is 0 m ·016 in diameter at the opening, and 0 m ·052 in depth ; the lateral groovings show that it was hollowed by a hard stone, worked round the interior by some appliance that wore away the haematite. On the outside three vertical cartouches are engraved side by side. The first ⬚, is the prenomen of Amenôthes III. The second contained the nomen of the same king, but during the religious revolution it was so thoroughly erased that now it is only possible to read the beginning of the name of Amon ⬚. The last cartouche is that of Queen Tîyi ⬚, wife of this king.

42. Vase in Amazonite.—Vase in the hard stone called amazonite, green with some red and blue spots, height 0 m ·049, diameter at top 0 m. ·047, in the middle 0 m ·043, at the base 0 m ·036. The shape is the traditional one for jars of collyrium. Owing to the hardness of the material the vase has not been hollowed out to the same extent as the preceding one, A mere cylindrical cavity has been bored 0 m ·016 in diameter and 0 m ·042 in depth. (Pl. VI, Fig. 1.)

On the outside is engraved very slightly, the tool having barely scratched the stone, the two cartouches of Amenôthes III.

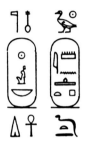

The upper rim is partly broken away.

43. Glass Vases.—Small vase in white glass, height 0 m ·065, measuring 0 m ·046 in diameter at the opening, 0 m ·052 in the middle, and 0 m ·038 at the foot. It was broken in several pieces, but it has been possible to reconstruct it almost completely. (Pl. V, Fig. 2.) The glass, of a mean thickness of 5 millimetres, must originally have been transparent, but with time it has become somewhat opaque; in the thinner portions it presents a slightly violet tint denoting the use of manganese to some considerable extent for whitening it during the process of manufacture. The shape is a rounded body, the neck short and widening slightly, a large opening with a plain curved border, the foot shallow. There is no ornamentation.

The fragments of two other vases in white glass were found. One of these is the neck of a bottle 0 m ·04 high; the other, 0 m ·06 high, is part of the body of a vase more elongated than that described above, and must have been similar in shape to the vase in glazed pottery forming part of the signs ⚥ on page 36.

STATUETTES OF THE GOD BES.

Among the pieces demanding special notice must be placed **two** figurines, in glazed pottery, of the god Bes: a form of Horus, who chases evil spirits and guards against sorcery. It is difficult to discover the object for which these figures were made, for the god is not represented under his usual aspect, with hands on his hips as he is when intended for an amulet. As the figure of Bes is often employed as a decoration for furniture and articles of the toilette it may be supposed that these two figures were intended to be used as convenient receptacles for oddments of the toilet table, although the cups they carry would scarcely hold more than a few pins.

44. The first Statuette is 0 m ·102 in height, the socle, rounded at the back, measures 0 m ·035 by 0 m ·038; the god is 0 m ·04 wide across the shoulders and thighs. (Pl. III, Fig. 3.) Bes is represented with his usual grotesque figure: a broad round head with low prominent forehead. flat nose, protruding lips and no chin, great round eyes with eyebrows strongly arched, wrinkled cheeks, lion's ears, hair resembling a mane more than anything else, ending in a point on the back. The belly is distended, the dorsal column is inflected outwards, from it spring five strongly marked ribs, and it is prolonged into an animal's tail which reaches to the ground. This deformed trunk is supported on two bow legs, short and massive, ending in huge feet. The swollen, ill-proportioned arms in front of the chest meet to support a circular dish; this vessel is slightly tilted and the hollow at the top is very shallow.

45. The second Statuette is 0 m ·09 in height and 0 m ·036 broad at the shoulders. (Pl. III, Fig. 1.) The type is somewhat similar, but of less careful workmanship; the differences to be observed are that the tongue of the god is hanging out, his hair terminates in a short plait, turned up at the end, the ribs are not indicated; the cup held by the god has a spout, and in the middle is placed some small round object indistinctly rendered. An attempt was made to embellish this statuette, which is in green glaze, with black; thus the eyes and the right ear have been painted, but the colour having run and formed blots behind the head, this ornamentation was not continued.

46. Models of Fruit.—In order to ensure a supply of food for the deceased, models were placed in the tomb representing bunches of grapes, in glazed pottery, of which the green colour has now disappeared. They are ovoid, covered either by squares formed of intersecting lines engraved on them, or by small circles in imitation of the grapes, obtained by re-working the squares, or by a mixture of the two forms. (Pl. IV, Figs. 1 and 3.)

Some of these objects have evidently been moulded in two parts. At the side furthest from the point there is generally a ring for suspension. Sometimes the ring forms part of a shank which was fixed into the bunch, sometimes it is a hole bored in a small piece of plastic material added to the model, and in some cases it is a bead attached with blue glass. The fifteen bunches found vary in size, the largest is 0 m ·05 in height and 0 m ·03 in diameter. The dimensions graduate to the smallest, which is only 0 m ·03 high and 0 m ·018 in diameter.

47. Models of Knives.—Seven imitation knives, in limestone, of the same form ⤳ as those used by butchers ; they are implements placed at the disposal of the deceased for slaying and cutting up any animals that he might require for food. (Pl. IV., Fig. 2.) Their length varies from 0 m ·138 to 0 m ·168 ; their breadth from 0 m ·022 to 0 m ·033. It is only their outlines that resemble knives made of bronze, and they are neither sharp nor pointed.

48. Models of Boomerangs.—Fourteen models of boomerangs or curved sticks for killing birds. The deceased could make use of these in the Other World to obtain food, or merely for the pleasure of sport. They are in glazed pottery, but the green colour is much faded, and the slight ornamentation drawn in black on the examples reproduced (Pl. VII, Figs. 2, 3, 4), is also scarcely visible. There are two types of these weapons. In the first the two extremities are rounded, and the section of the whole length is a very flat oval ; eight of these have been found in lengths ranging from 0 m ·120 to 0 m ·148. The six specimens of the second type are rather more bent, the end nearest the broadened part is rounded, but the haft is of round section and is square at the end. Their length is from 0 m ·120 to 0 m ·158.

49. Handle of a Tool.—Handle of a tool in cedar wood, length 0 m ·16, which must have been left in the tomb by a workman. (Pl. VIII.) The section is an oval of 0 m ·026 by 0 m ·023 in diameter, and the edges are slightly concave. One end is rounded, the other is cut straight and has a groove 0 m ·014 in breadth, and 0 m ·024 in depth, for fixing a blade such as a carpenter's chisel.

50. **Awl.**—Bronze awl ; without a handle ; a squared stem 0 m ·104 in length, pointed at one end. The maximum breadth, 0 m ·004, occurs at about two-thirds of the length. (Pl. VII, Fig. 6.)

51. **Stone for sharpening.**—Block of hard slatey schist, black, which must have been used to sharpen tools. Length 0 m ·178, breadth 0 m ·032, depth 0 m ·02 ; two of the faces are flat, parallel, and terminated in semi-circles.

52. **Label.**—Small label in cedar wood, of the form ⌂, pierced with a hole at the top, measuring 0 m ·033 by 0 m ·021. On it is this inscription in hieratic, written with black ink "sawdust of the tree *nozem*."

53. **Head of a Goose in silver.**—Fragment of some object, the purpose of which I cannot conjecture. A silver plaque, hollowed into a channel and bent into a quarter of a circle, has fixed to it a small silver tube ; one end of this tube is carried through the open beak of a goose's head, the other end is closed by a strip of bronze ; the top of the head was inlaid. The length is 0 m ·08 the breadth 0 m ·012.

54. **Discs in bronze gilt.**—Two discs, 0 m ·047 in diameter, in bronze gilt, pierced with four holes in order to attach them to some unknown object. They are slightly convex, and stamped in relief to imitate some flower of the composite order, with a central knob and numerous petals radiating all round it.

55. **Discs in gold.**—Gold disc, 0 m ·035 in diameter, on which is figured in relief a five-pointed star. It is pierced with four holes for attachment. (Pl. VII, Fig. 8.)

56. **Small gold Disc.**—Only 0 m ·016 in diameter. Like the decorations

above in bronze gilt, it represents a flower, but the central knob is larger in comparison and the petals much shorter. it is pierced with three holes.

57. **Mane in gold.**—Gold leaf crimped and engraved, it must have over-laid a figure of a lion either in wood or glazed pottery. The length is 0 m ·12, and the breadth also 0 m ·12. The whole surface is covered in imitation of tufts of hair arranged round a lock on the forehead, between the two hollows for the ears.

58. **Copper Plaques and Nails.**—Several small copper plaques of irregular form, one of which is reproduced. (Pl. VIII, Fig. 1.) They have been used to consolidate wooden objects. The bronze nails, length from 14 to 26 millimetres, are roughly wrought ; several of them still adhere to the plaques, and served to secure them to the objects to be strengthened or supported.

PLATES.

PLATE I.

TOMB OF QUEEN TÎYI.

PLATE II.

THE TOMB EXCAVATORS, 1907 (R. TO L.: E. ARYTON, T. DAVIS, WITH A. WEIGALL AND WIFE.) *(Courtesy Birmingham City Library.)*

PLATE III.

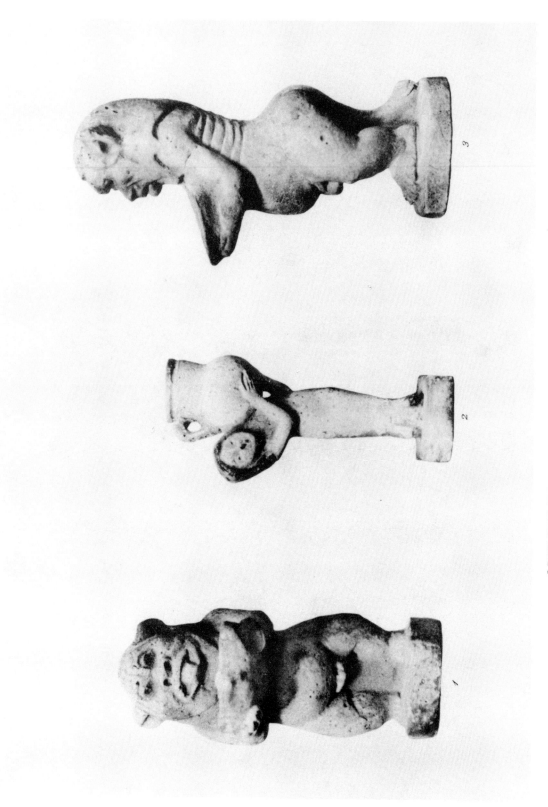

OBJECTS FOUND IN THE TOMB OF QUEEN TÎYI.

PLATE IV.

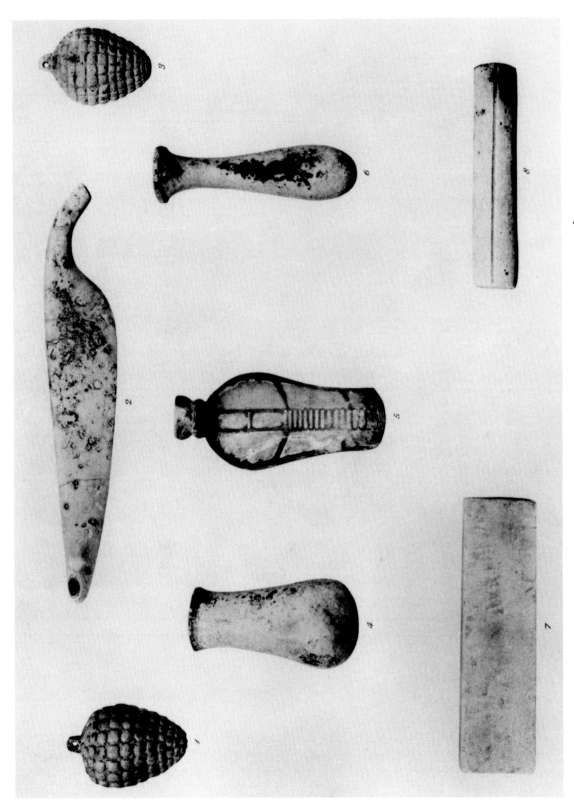

OBJECTS FOUND IN THE TOMB OF QUEEN TÎYI.

PLATE V.

OBJECTS FOUND IN THE TOMB OF QUEEN TÎYI.

PLATE VI.

OBJECTS FOUND IN THE TOMB OF QUEEN TÎYI.

PLATE VII.

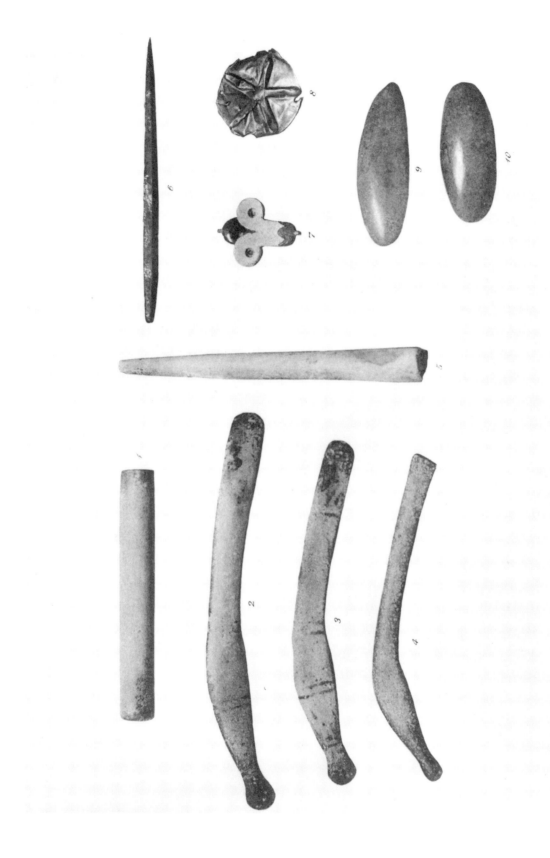

SMALL OBJECTS FOUND IN THE TOMB OF QUEEN TÎYI.

PLATE VIII.

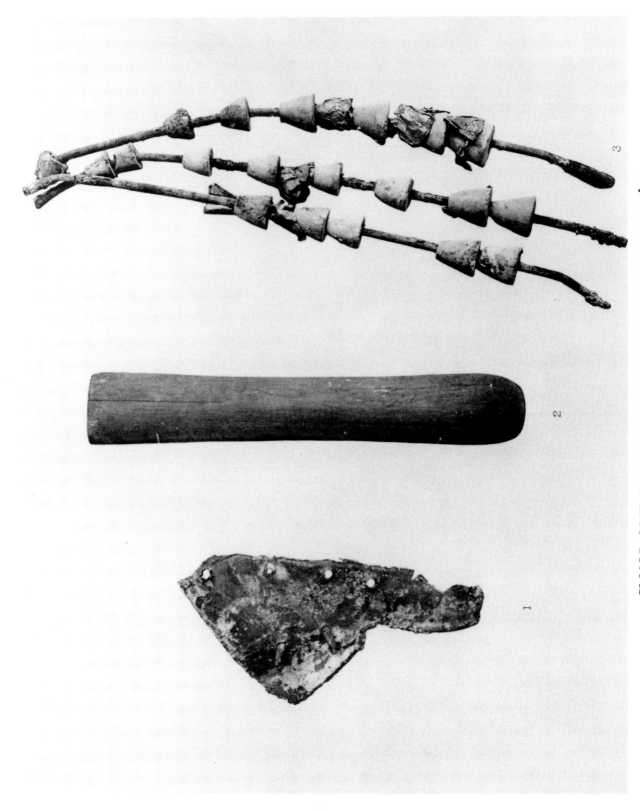

SMALL OBJECTS FOUND IN THE TOMB OF QUEEN TÎYI.

PLATE IX.

FOUR ALABASTER HEADS OF QUEEN TÎYI.

PLATE X.

FOUR ALABASTER HEADS OF QUEEN TÎYI.

PLATE XI.

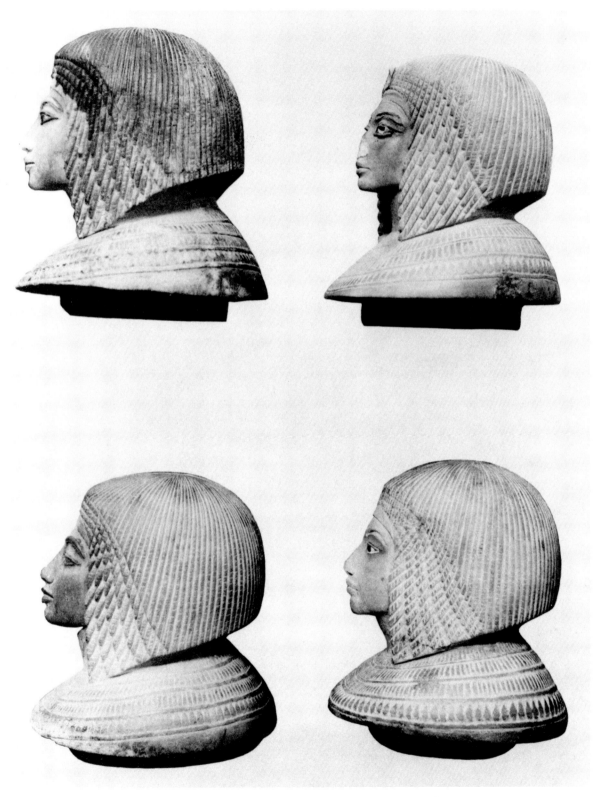

FOUR ALABASTER HEADS OF QUEEN TÎYI.

PLATE XII.

ALABASTER PORTRAIT HEAD OF QUEEN TÎYI -NATURAL SIZE.

PLATE XIII.

ALABASTER PORTRAIT HEAD OF QUEEN TÎYI -NATURAL SIZE.

PLATE XIV.

ALABASTER PORTRAIT HEAD OF QUEEN TIYI -NATURAL SIZE.

PLATE XV.

ALABASTER PORTRAIT HEAD OF QUEEN TÎYI -NATURAL SIZE.

PLATE XVI.

ALABASTER PORTRAIT HEAD OF QUEEN TÎYI -NATURAL SIZE.

PLATE XVII.

ALABASTER PORTRAIT HEAD OF QUEEN TÎYI -NATURAL SIZE.

PLATE XVIII.

ALABASTER PORTRAIT HEAD OF QUEEN TÎYI -NATURAL SIZE.

PLATE XIX.

ALABASTER PORTRAIT HEAD OF QUEEN TÎYI -NATURAL SIZE.

PLATE XX.

CANOPIC JARS OF QUEEN TÎYI.

70

PLATE XXI.

CANOPIC JARS OF QUEEN TÎYI.

PLATE XXII.

IMPERIAL CROWN OF QUEEN TÎYI.

PLATE XXIII.

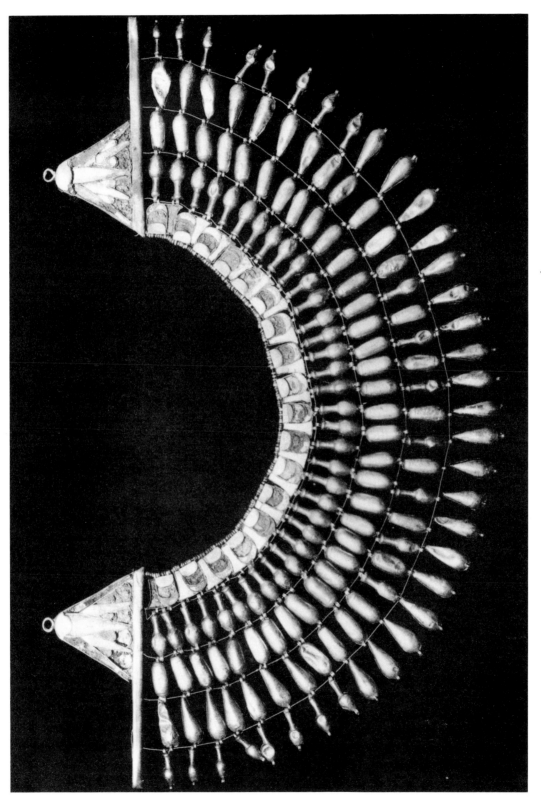

GOLD NECKLACE OF QUEEN TÎYI.

PLATE XXIV.

CORNER BRICKS.

PLATE XXV.

BRONZE WEDGES.

PLATE XXVI.

ENTRANCE TO THE TOMB OF QUEEN TÎYI.

PLATE XXVII.

PLATE XXVIII.

SEPUCHRAL CHAMBER SHOWING SHRINE (DESTROYED)

PLATE XXIX.

SEPUCHRAL CHAMBER SHOWING COFFIN AND CANOPIC JARS.

PLATE XXX.

PANEL COVERED IN GOLD FOIL. SHOWING PORTRAIT OF QUEEN

PLATE XXXI.

SEPULCHRAL CHAMBER. FRAGMENT OF SHRINE.

PLATE XXXII.

COFFIN IN SEPULCHRAL CHAMBER.

PLATE XXXIII.

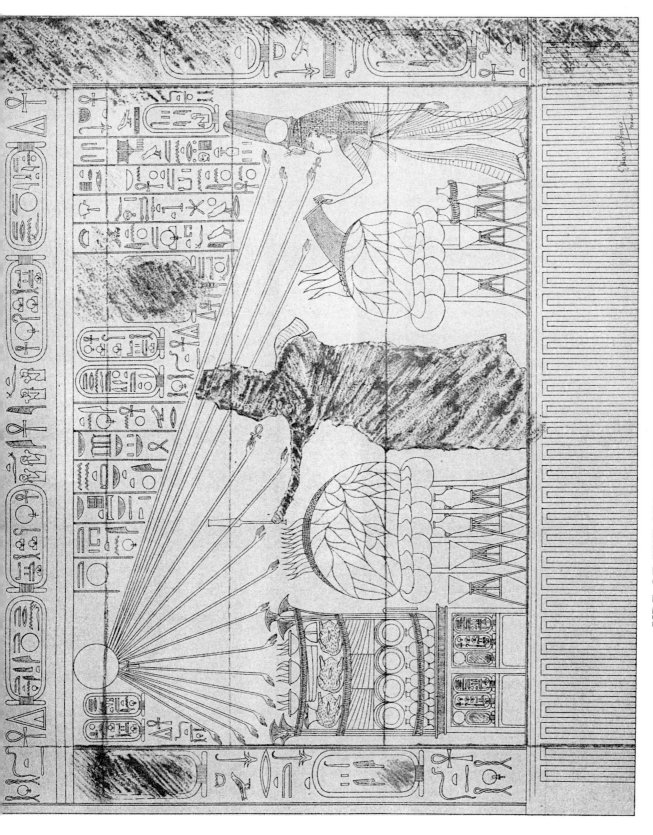

SIDE OF THE SEPULCHRAL CANOPY SHOWING THE FIGURE.

Painted by E. HAROLD JONES

PLATE XXXIV.

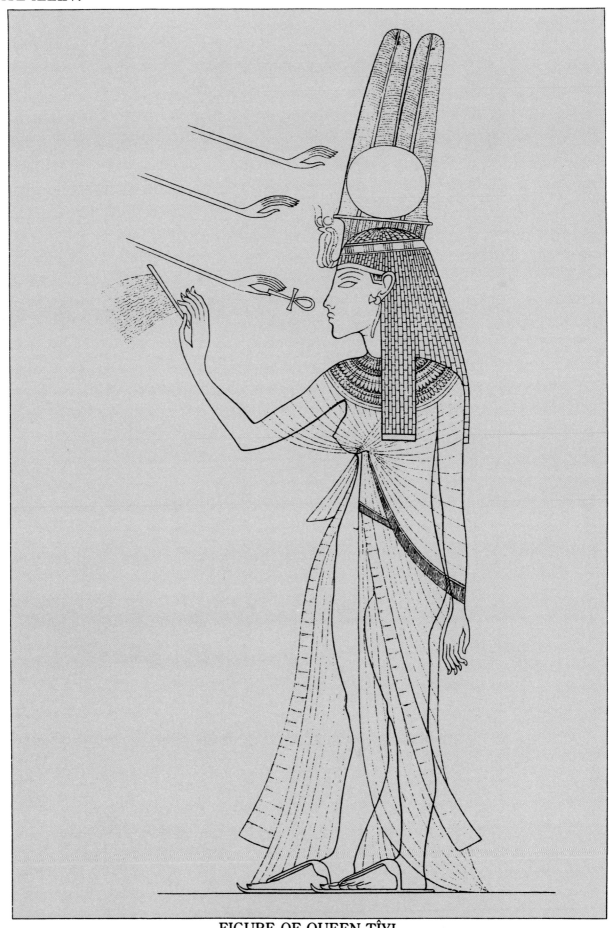

FIGURE OF QUEEN TÎYI.
Painted by E. HAROLD JONES

PLATE XXXV.

RIGHT-HAND POST AND BEAMS COVERED WITH STUCCO
OVERLAID WITH GOLD, FROM SEPUCHRAL CANOPY.

Painted by E. HAROLD JONES

PLATE XXXVI.

HEAD OF QUEEN TÎYI.

FROM A STATUETTE, FOUND BY PROFESSOR PETRIE AT SINAI.

86

PLATE XXXVII.

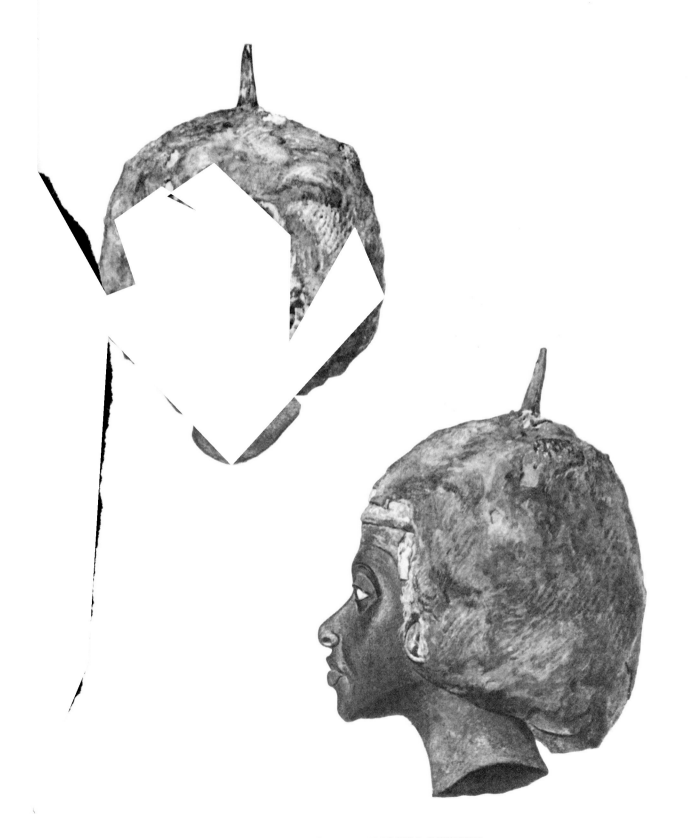

HEAD OF UNKNOWN QUEEN.

(Found in Fayum, purchased by Berlin Egyptian Museum.)
Published for comparison with Queen Tîyi.

87

PLATE XXXVIII.

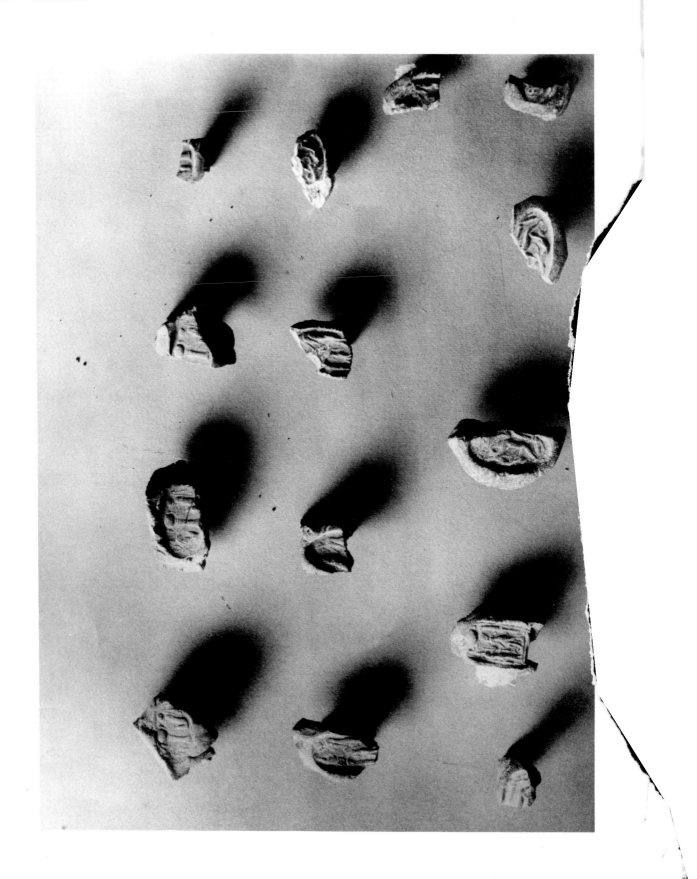

PLATE XXXIX.

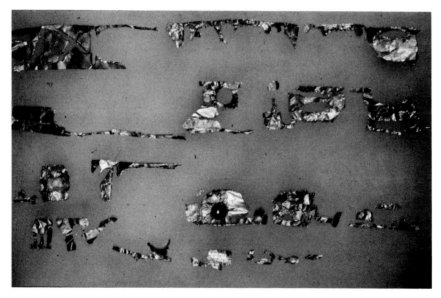

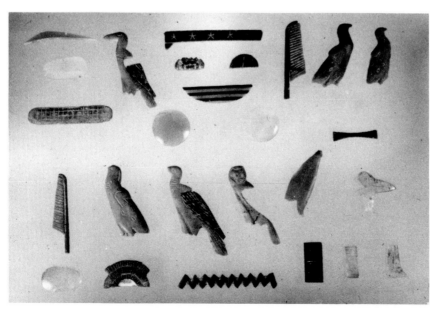

GOLD FOIL AND INLAYS FROM BANDS B. AND C. OF COFFIN.

89

Originally Published in 1910
by Archibald Constable and Co., Ltd.
London